Cricket for Americans

Cricket for Americans:
Playing and Understanding the Game

Tom Melville

With A Preface by Ian Chappell

Bowling Green State University Popular Press
Bowling Green, OH 43403

Sports and Culture Series
General Editors
  Douglas Noverr
  Larry Ziewacz

Cover design by Gary Dumm

"had your fill of cricket, Mr. Barnes?
No, son, I've had my share, but never my fill."
—82-year-old Syd Barnes to Jeff Stollmeyer

Contents

Acknowledgements

The long road this work has traveled from idea to printed page would not have been possible without the help and generosity of many people. Time has now come to express, in alphabetical order, my heartfelt thanks to them all.

To Don Bradman for the photo of himself at fighting weight (plate 15); Simon Cobley of Orion Publishing for permission to reprint, from Tom Smith's *Cricket Umpiring and Scoring*, the illustration on page 26; Patrick Eagar for his fine action photos (plates 2, 3, 4 & 5); Ghulam Mustafa Khan of the Board of Control for Cricket in Pakistan for information on cricket in his country; Murray Haines, the dedicated secretary of the C.C. Morris Cricket Library for help in making available the invaluable resources of this fine library; Kate Hempsall of the Surrey County Cricket club for the photo of Kennington Oval (plate 13); John Jameson of the MCC for the generous permission to reprint the official Laws of Cricket; Hayward Kidson, of the United Cricket Board of South Africa for information on the game in South Africa; Ian Kerville of Commercial Communications for the fine photo of the Melbourne Cricket Ground (plate 14); Stephanie Lawrence of the ICC for information on the workings of her organization; Mrs. T.J. MacDonald of the IWCC for information on women's cricket; Mueen-ud-Din Hameed for his photo of Gaddafi Stadium (plate 19); S.S. Perera for his material on cricket in Sir Lanka; Andrew Sealy of the West Indian Cricket Board of Control for information on cricket in the Caribbean and for the photo of Kensington Oval (plate 16); Alan Smith of the TCCB for information on cricket in England; R.E. Steiner of the ACB for the helpful material on cricket in Australia; Ms Vida Tong for the fine photos from her newspaper the Johannesburg *Star* (plates 1, 6, 7, 8, 17 & 18).

i

ii Cricket for Americans

Finally, I would like to express a special thanks to Ian Chappell for his wonderful preface, to Pat Browne and her attentive staff at the Popular Press for putting everything together, as well as to Georgia Jung and the rest of the staff of the Cedarburg Public Library for their patient help with what must have seemed like an interminable stream of interlibrary loan requests.

They kept open my "supply line" to the vast world of cricket information.

Preface

A television producer once gave me an insight into how frustrating cricket must be to people who aren't brought up on the game.

"How," he said, "can you expect a visiting American to be anything but confused by cricket, when in the space of a few minutes of commentary, you've referred to that revered stretch of land as the pitch, the wicket, the track, the strip and the deck?"

He had a valid point, but unfortunately for Americans, opportunities to get their own back are restricted. I played baseball for many years and I've been an avid follower ever since I was old enough to realise a mantlepiece wasn't The Mick getting a large chunk of one and depositing yet another ball in the rightfield seats at Yankee stadium. I've even experienced the satisfaction of explaining to a Mets fan, who arrived late at Shea stadium, how the fascinating duel between Dwight Gooden and Nolan Ryan was progressing in game 5 of the 1986 National League Championship Series.

"Goddam, how do you know so much about the game from 7,500 miles away?" he exploded, after I'd related how Dr. K and The Ryan Express were dominating the hitters.

It's true there are a lot of similarities between cricket and baseball. Both have a batter who faces a ball propelled in his direction at roughly the same speed and there's a backstop (wicketkeeper/catcher) waiting to tidy up if the batter misses, or declines to offer at the missile. Caught is a common method of dismissal in both games and the ball is practically the same size and weight.

However, because of American expediency and English eccentricity, there's one vital difference in the two games. Baseball has an inbuilt mechanism that ensures nothing can stay the same for any longer than a six count, while in cricket, if you deliver six balls (an over) and nothing happens, the bowler is accorded a standing ovation.

Such a momentous occasion in cricket is called "bowling a maiden over." Without a very convincing explanation an American could come to the conclusion that it's not surprising cricketers practise assiduously on Tuesday and Thursday nights. Other cricket sayings like "fielding in slips" and "between the covers" can be equally misread, but then so too can "he's struck out," if your knowledge of baseball is restricted to a hazy notion that maybe Joe DiMaggio and Marilyn Monroe dated occasionally.

This is where Tom Melville's book, *Cricket For Americans*, bridges the gap. Tom has taken the game of cricket and cleverly explained it, making good use of baseball terminology. Hopefully, after reading Tom's book, an American who takes the wrong turn on his way to Bondi beach and arrives at the Sydney Cricket Ground (SCG), will not be totally disappointed when he finally sees a cricketer bowl a maiden over.

As a lover of both cricket and baseball I hope Tom's audacious exercise succeeds. Having enjoyed reading his book, I now won't put my foot in it by asking a visitor to the SCG, "mate, how the bloody hell do you know so much about cricket, coming from America?"

Ian Chappell
Former Captain, Australian Test Team.

Introduction

So you'd like to learn about cricket?

Congratulations! You've chosen one of the world's great sports, easy to understand, fun to play and watch, and one with a rich and diverse international history and tradition.

If you're like most other Americans who have ever been curious about England's national pastime, however, you may have already discovered that cricket's not exactly the most approachable sport, particularly for the total newcomer.

Who hasn't heard stories about American tourists frustrated to tears by their inability to make heads nor tails of the match they watched while in England? Or the American businessman who couldn't understand a single word of what his Australian clients were saying when their conversation turned to the game?

Nor is this situation easily remedied with a visit to the bookstore or library, where an American may find plenty of publications on cricket, but none that presume its readers are from a non-cricket background.

This work is intended to fill this small, but noticeable gap in the sports literature by providing a short, concise, all purpose cricket guide that's been specifically written to help Americans through their first experience with cricket, in whatever form that experience may take.

Here an American teacher, interested in trying the game in his or her physical education class, can find a complete beginners program.

An American journalist covering the game for the first time can find a clear and non-technical explanation of cricket terminology.

An American librarian asked for information about the game's rules or organization will find a handy, concise, yet authoritative reference source on the subject, just as the American traveler planning to take in a match, will find a detailed preview of what to expect.

2 Cricket for Americans

In short, the work is intended to serve as a one-stop resource for any American who, for whatever reason, simply wants to know about the workings of this great world sport.

As a work written by an American specifically for Americans, it frequently makes comparisons to baseball and other American sports, the most accessible and convenient context for understanding cricket, and, above all, has attempted to let the game speak for itself from its most basic and translatable features as a bat and ball sport.

Enjoy the game.

Chapter One
How Do You Play this Game?

There weren't too many people in my small Midwestern town who knew much about cricket back when I was beginning to play the game.

So I'd gather up my cricket equipment, find a vacant baseball diamond, and often spend my summer evenings practicing by myself, usually bowling at stumps I'd pitched just behind home plate, over after over, trying to hone my line and length until the falling shadows made it too dark to even see the ball.

At first, all this went on pretty much unnoticed by the locals, but it wasn't long before my solitary practice sessions began to arouse more than passing interest. Each evening more after dinner joggers, bikers and dog walkers began to stop, look at, and ponder this mysterious ritual that had sprouted up on their neighborhood ball diamond.

Arms length curiosity eventually came to direct interrogation, and soon I was answering, as I would almost every evening for the rest of the summer, those questions I've been answering for Americans ever since: "What's the name of this game? How's it played? Is it fun?"

I don't know if I became a better cricket player by the end of that summer, but I certainly discovered how naturally curious Americans were about cricket. What's more, I also discovered it didn't take most Americans long to realize that cricket, far from being the complex, arcane mystery they'd been led to believe was, in fact, a fairly simple, straight-forward bat and ball game made of the same basic ball playing features they knew from baseball.

Cricket, of course, is a game that applies these features in its own unique, and sometimes very different, ways, but as we'll see in this chapter, not so different that any American, asked for a thumbnail description of the game, couldn't answer the same way

4 Cricket for Americans

Willie Mays is said to have replied when asked the same question about baseball; its just a game where "You throw the ball and I hit it. I hit it and you catch it."

Field of Other Dreams

Cricket's often called the "meadow game."

Step onto just about any cricket ground anywhere around the world and you'll understand how it got this name. You won't find here a playing area cluttered with backstops, bases, pitching mounds or scarred with a cut out infield. Just an open, circular expanse of closely cropped turf, completely encircled by either a chalk or rope boundary line. There's no official size for a cricket ground, though the ones used by the pros are seldom less than 150 yards in diameter, and some as wide as 200 yards or more.

The only physical objects you'll notice on a cricket ground are two sets of three short, wooden poles, standing upright, facing each other, in the center of the playing area, 22 yards apart.

These are the *wickets*. Officially 28" high, 9" wide, and holding two small, cylindrical 4 3/8" pieces of molded wood, called *bails*, in grooves on their tops, the wickets, with bails, function, for all practical purposes, as the "bases" of cricket, as we'll shortly explain.

Four feet in front of, and running parallel to each wicket is a twelve foot chalk line called the *popping crease*. This crease, also called the *batting crease*, is, in effect, the cricket batters "safe line." Anytime the batter's completely over this line, away from the wicket, he can be put out. Anytime he's got some part of his body behind the line, he's always safe.

Running back towards the wicket at right angles to the popping crease, 8' 8" apart, are two eight foot chalk lines, called the *return creases*. They demarcate the operating area for the cricket "pitcher" (that's not what he's actually called, but we'll get to that a little later).

A fourth line, running parallel to, and four feet behind, the popping crease, joins the return creases. Rule changes in the sixties have effectively rendered this line, called the *bowling crease*, obsolete, but, by custom, it's still usually marked, if only for the convenience of having a line on which the wickets can be placed.

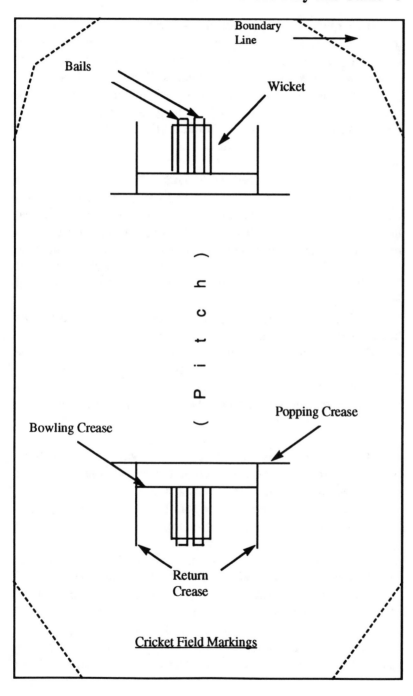

Boundary
Line

Bails

Wicket

(P i t c h)

Popping Crease

Bowling Crease

Return
Crease

Cricket Field Markings

The stretch of turf between the wickets, and about as wide as the return creases, officially called the *pitch*, though commonly, if incorrectly, also called the "wicket," is always manicured to a golf-green smoothness, the reason for which we'll also explain shortly.

Because its expensive to maintain a traditional turf pitch in this condition, some clubs, especially on the amateur and school level, have, in recent years, started to install artificial pitches, which look something like a strip of astroturf.

Tools of the Trade

Cricket, as we've said, is a bat and ball game. It uses a hard ball that, officially, can't be any heavier than 5 1/2 ounces, and no larger in circumference than 8 13/16 inches. Although the blood red cricket ball, with its single stitched seam down the middle, may look very different from a baseball, the two are actually made of basically the same material; alternating layers of cork and wool covered with leather.

Cricket's most distinctive piece of equipment, of course, is its large, paddle-shaped bat.

They're all made of willow, can be any weight, but can't be any longer than 38 inches or wider than 4 1/4 inches. A top-of-the-line model, hand made from the best quality willow and outfitted with a good cane, steel-spring handle, is a virtual work of art.

Clearly, this isn't a tool intended for any game that will sacrifice it to the one-shot requirements of a broken-bat single. It's designed to keep its user up at bat for extended periods of time, guiding, controlling, directing each and every pitch not for one or two, but, as we'll see, dozens of runs at a time.

Americans who see cricket for the first time are usually surprised at how much protective equipment a cricket batter must wear.

Why does he have to have on a pair of large, padded leg guards that look something like field hockey goal-keeping pads? Or a pair of gloves padded on the back of the fingers and palms? Or a helmet often outfitted with a football-like face guard?

The answer is very simple. In cricket, it's not illegal for the "pitcher" to hit the batter with the ball. So the batter wears leg guards to protect his lower legs (where, as we'll see, he's most likely to get hit), batting gloves to protect him from pitches that may "jam" him, and a helmet that protects his entire head.

One piece of protective equipment you won't see in cricket—fielding gloves, because, with one exception, they're illegal to use, a requirement that doesn't in the least handicap a cricketer from making as sparkling, though perhaps not as routinely consistent, fielding plays as his glove wearing counterpart in baseball.

The one fielder who is allowed to wear gloves, the *wicket-keeper*, a cricket position, in purpose and function, identical to the baseball catcher, doesn't wear one, but two flat, long-cuffed leather gloves, that look something like the shallow pocketed baseball gloves of the twenties and thirties. The wicket-keeper—who also has on a pair of leg-guards, but, for reasons we'll also explain later, no face mask or chest protector—wears two gloves because he usually has to make low, two handed basket catches similar to the way a baseball catcher plays balls in the dirt. How, you might ask, can the wicket-keeper throw with a glove on each hand? The answer is, he doesn't have to. There are no stolen bases or double plays in cricket that require a free hand for long throwing.

The traditional cricket uniform has long been a pair of immaculate white (or cream) trousers, long or short-sleeved shirt and a pair of white cleated shoes, conspicuously free of any player names, numbers or splashy logos.

Teams will display their individual club insignia on their caps, which look like low-brimmed baseball caps, and club colors on the trim or embroidery of their "tennis" style, cable knit wool sweaters.

Having both teams wear basically the same color uniforms is never a problem in cricket because, as we'll see, in a cricket match the opposing teams are never all on the field at the same time.

Batsmen Up!

The story goes that a famous cricket player was once asked how he would play a particularly tricky type of pitch.

"How would *I* play it?" he gruffly replied, "Why, I would put bat to ball, Sir, bat to ball!"

When you come right down to it, that's pretty much what cricket's all about. Like baseball, its basically a matter of making contact with a pitched ball, and the more often the better.

But when a cricket batter (or "batsman," as he's officially called in cricket) comes to bat, taking up his normal position on top of the popping crease and a little to the side of his wicket, ready to face the "pitcher," throwing from the other wicket, he knows he's going to be batting under conditions very different from anything he'll find in baseball.

To begin with, the cricket batter knows that no matter how often he swings at, and misses, the ball, he's never going to "strike out," because there are no balls or strikes in cricket, just as he knows that any ball he does hit—even ones that go sideways or backwards—will be "fair," because there's no "foul territory" in cricket.

He knows he'll always be batting with a partner, who plays at the opposite wicket, bat in hand. Only one of them will actually be hitting the ball at any given time, but they must work together to score runs.

The cricket batter also knows he doesn't have to run after hitting the ball if he doesn't want to, but, if he does decide to run, he knows he and his partner only have to run as far as the opposite wicket. Once they've both made it over their respective popping creases, they've got themselves a run. That's all there is to it. No 360 foot, four-base circumnavigation, just a 60-foot straight line scamper to the other wicket.

What's more, he and his partner can continue running back and forth from wicket to wicket this way, after hitting the ball, as often as they feel they can do so safely, and will score another run each and every time they switch.

Though he and his partner, like all cricket batters, must carry their bats *with* them when running, this is really no disadvantage. The bat's considered an extension of the batters arm, so all he has to do is touch the bat down over the popping crease to be safe.

He knows his team will get six automatic runs each and every time he or anyone else hits a fly ball over the boundary line (this is something like a "home run" in cricket), four automatic runs each and every time he or anyone hits a ground ball over the boundary line. The batters don't even have to ceremonially trot out these runs, they just stay where they are and continue batting, which they can do until the fielding team can get them out.

Our cricket batter knows he can even score runs without hitting the ball. He and his partner can run, and run as often as they want, if the ball gets past the wicket-keeper (called a *bye*, something like a cricket "passed ball"), or if the ball deflects far enough off his batting pads (runs scored this way are called *leg byes*).

Out!

If you're beginning to think, at this point, that cricket's predominantly a batter's game, you'd certainly be right. But not everything about the game is stacked in the batters favor. The fielding team also knows they have plenty of ways to get the batter out.

To begin with, they know that if their "pitcher" can get so much as one pitch (actually called a "delivery" in cricket) past the batter, hit his wicket, and knock off at least one bail, the batter will be out, right on the spot (the batter, in this instance, is out *bowled*, something like a cricket "strike out").

They also know the batter will be a "goner" if he flies out (out, *caught*, just like baseball), hits his own wicket and knocks off at least one bail while batting, even if he does this accidentally (out, *hit wicket*), or if he blocks a pitch from hitting his wicket with his body, even if he also does this unintentionally (out, *leg before wicket*, always abbreviated LBW).

The fielders can also pick up an out if they can field a ball on which the batters are running, throw it, hit the wicket towards which one of them is running, and knock off a bail, before he can get over the popping crease. The fielders can also get the batter out this way (called a *run out*, something like being caught "off base" in cricket) by holding the ball in their hand and hitting the wicket, but *never* by "tagging"the batter with the ball. The fielders can run out either batter, at either wicket, but *only* one at a time. There's no "double play" in cricket.

They can also get a batter out if, at any time, he goes completely over the popping crease trying to hit the ball (perfectly legal), misses, and can't get back before their wicket-keeper grabs the ball and hits his wicket. The batter in this case is said to be out *stumped*, something like a cricket "pick off."

Now and then the fielders may even have the good fortune of seeing a batter get himself out, if he happens to touch a ball that's in play (out, *handled the ball*), hit a pitch twice (out, *hit the ball-twice*), or intentionally interfere with a fielder (out, *obstructing the field*).

Best of all, the fielders know that, although the batter can bat until out, once he is out, he'll only get, as we'll explain shortly, at the most, one more time at bat

On "The Mound"

Up to this point we've been calling the fielder who throws to the batter the "pitcher." That, however, is not what he's called in cricket. He's called a *bowler* and must follow a number of special rules.

The bowler must have at least some part of his front foot behind the popping crease and some part of his back foot inside the return creases at the time he releases the ball. Any pitch not thrown this way, called a *no ball*, results in one penalty run for the batting team and must be taken over.

The bowler must also "bowl" the ball, not "throw" it. That means, he must throw the ball with a straight arm, locked, at the elbow. He positively cannot throw the ball with a baseball-like "whiplash" arm motion. If he does, he'll also be called for a no ball.

Finally, the bowler must throw the ball so that it is at least within reach of the batter. Any pitch the umpires believe is out of reach of the batter, called a *wide*, also results in one penalty run for the batting team and must also be taken over.

The bowler is, however, allowed to take as long a run up as he wants when bowling, and can bowl the ball to the batter not only on the fly, but also on the bounce, which he will almost always try to do, on one bounce, since a ball thrown this way is the hardest to hit.

This explains why the pitch must be manicured to a golf-green smoothness (to eliminate erratic, dangerous bounces) and also why the batter wears protective leg guards (most balls will be bowled to the batter on a single, knee-high bounce).

The Over

You may remember that we said cricket batting is always done in pairs.

To give both batters a chance to hit, the direction of the bowling is reversed, every six pitches. That is, after a bowler has thrown six fair pitches towards one wicket, another fielder takes the ball, goes to the opposite wicket, and bowls six times in the other direction. This change of bowling direction (called an *over*) continues every six pitches, throughout the match. The fielding team can change bowlers after every over if they want, and can even "bring back" someone who's bowled before, so long as no-one bowls two overs in succession.

This also means, of course, that the wicket-keeper must shuttle back and forth from wicket to wicket at the end of each over so that he's always positioned behind the wicket opposite the bowler.

Wins, Draws and Ties

A cricket match (like tennis, always called a "match," never a "game"), lasts only one, or, at the most, two innings.

This is because all eleven members of the batting team (the official number of players allowed on a cricket team) must come to bat and all except one be put out, one after another, before the fielding team can come up. The very last batter, left at the end, with no more partners, doesn't have to be put out because, as we've said, no-one can bat alone.

When the fielding team comes up, they, in turn, will bat through their entire order the same way. This would constitute a one innings match. If the teams are playing a two innings match, they would each bat twice. In either case, the team with the most runs, is the winner.

It shouldn't be hard to understand why it sometimes takes a long time to finish a cricket match. In a two innings match, a total of forty-four batters may come up, and all can bat until they're out, something that usually won't be possible unless the match is extended over several days.

Like a sprawling Russian novel, cricket just happens to be one of these expressions of humanity whose intricacies of plot and variety of characters need an extended period of time to unfold.

The team that's up first, for example, may use up most or all of the first days playing time sometimes rushing, sometimes crawling, but always spiritually moving, towards the safe harbor of a large first innings total; the other team all, or most, of the second days playing time in a Homeric quest to catch up to and strike out beyond this total. Then, trying to close each other out, another day or two of attacks, counter-attacks, ambushes and holding actions, over the second innings.

And even with this much time allocated, it still might not be possible to completely finish the match, in which case it would be declared a *draw*, the official result whenever a match, for whatever reason, cannot be played completely through, *regardless* of the score. If the match had finished with the scores dead even, it would have been a *tie*, not a draw.

Because these traditional matches tend to be so long, and often end up without a result, a shorter, more time controlled type of cricket can be played, called *limited overs* cricket, or, because this type of match is usually finished in a single days play, *one day cricket*.

In this type of cricket, which has become increasingly popular with cricket fans all over the world, each batter is still allowed to bat until he's out, but his team as a whole can only bat for a pre-determined number of overs. If two teams, for example, agree to play a forty over match, this means neither team can bat for more than forty overs (or, if you prefer, 240 pitches), even if all their batters don't get up in that time.

With each team restricted in its time at bat, limited overs matches are also guaranteed to end in a definite result, never a draw.

Chapter Two
The Inner Game

Now that you know how cricket's played, you might be tempted to conclude that this must also be a pretty simple game on the strategic level.

After all, the batters just have to run a few yards back and forth to score runs, the fielders just have to stop, catch, and throw in the ball. No double plays, stolen bases or hit and runs.

Don't be fooled for one minute.

Behind this facade of stately, even languid serenity, a tense, dynamic, all-out battle is going on between opponents who have at their disposal as wide and sophisticated an array of tactics, ploys and stratagems as any big league baseball or professional football team.

The Captain

What's more, responsibility for guiding a cricket team through the tactical complexities of any given match lies solely and exclusively in the hands of its captain, who must make all these decisions under the fire of on-field play, rather than from the distant calm of a sideline or dugout.

Cricket clubs do have coaches and managers, but even on the professional level they're strictly behind-the-scenes personnel. Once a cricket match has started, and, in some circumstances, well before, the team captain, and he alone, assumes responsibility for everything from field placement to team motivation.

The closest thing we have to this in American sports is probably the "player coach," though the cricket captain, unlike some aging baseball or basketball veteran, who's just easing himself into a second career, is fully expected to lead by example with an occasional stint of breakthrough bowling or inspired spell of catch-up batting, the proverbial *captain's innings,* an expression in cricket playing countries that's passed into the street equivalent of our "showing true grit."

The individual delegated the highest of all cricket captaincies, that of his country's national (always called a *test*) team, virtually assumes, with the job, a sacred trusteeship of his nation's international prestige. If he happens to be successful in that role he might enjoy, like the record breaking captain of the West Indies, Clive Lloyd, greater notoriety than his country's prime minister. If not, he might find himself a virtual exile from his own land, something that actually befell Indian test captain Ajit Wadeckar for a while after his team was badly beaten in a series against England in the early seventies.

The Toss

Whether he's masterminding his nation's test team, or just calling the shots for a village eleven, every cricket captain begins his job with a coin toss.

If he wins, the first thing he has to do is decide whether to bat or field.

Because cricket is a game where the ball is almost always bounced to the batter, this decision will normally revolve around little else than the condition of the pitch.

If it's dry and fairly firm, the captain will probably bat first since the ball can normally be expected to bounce a little more evenly on a fresh, unused pitch than on one that's been slightly chopped up, which it would be by the time the other team has batted on it.

On the other hand, if there seems to be anything in the condition of the pitch that's likely to make batting difficult— an unusual amount of dampness, for example, that could induce slightly erratic bounces—he might prefer to put the other team in and let his bowlers have a go.

Now and then a captain may let the other team bat first as a matter of psychological convenience, preferring to know, when his team comes up, exactly how many runs they'll need to win. You're most likely to see this in limited overs matches where the games are too short to make any appreciable wear and tear on the pitch.

The Lineup

Let's say our captain decides to bat first. If he hasn't already done so, he must now put together his batting order, which, in its basic purpose and philosophy, isn't really that much different from a baseball lineup.

The first two batters, called the *openers*, are, like the lead off and number two batters in baseball, normally good contact hitters. They're usually a cricket team's most disciplined and technically sound batters, hard to get out because they're always very careful and selective in the way they play each and every pitch.

The openers primary objective is to "take the shine off the ball." That is, they want to gradually wear down their opponent's starting bowlers (who begin with a shiny new cricket ball) by carefully picking up a scampered single here, another there, patiently getting up a score the other batters on their team can build on.

The number three position in the batting order is usually reserved for a cricket team's best all-around batter, the player who's technically sound enough to play through the best bowlers, strong enough to punish the not-so-good ones, and versatile enough to adopt to everything in between.

With eight partners yet to come up, the number three batter's also given plenty of time to use his talent, enough to possibly put together a "big innings," one of those Herculean, one-man outputs of a hundred runs or more, that can, singlehandedly, put a team's score out of reach of the opposition.

The number four and five slots in the cricket lineup are usually occupied by the team's "big hitters." Like the "cleanup" batters in baseball, these are the players who may be somewhat questionable in technique, but once they get going, can usually be expected to hit for power, quite valuable if the top-of-the-order batters have gone down "cheaply" and the team has to stage a late innings rally, or, if it happens to be a limited overs, match make up a lot of runs in the few overs that might be left.

A team fortunate to have in its lineup a genuine *all rounder*, that is, a player multi-talented enough to hold a starting place as both a batter and bowler, will normally put him in the number six spot, followed, at number seven, by the wicket-keeper. Both the all rounder and wicket-keeper bat lower in the order to give them time to rest up from possibly long and tiring spells of bowling and wicket-keeping, which they'll need if their team has had to field first.

The bowlers usually occupy the final four spots in the lineup, for pretty much the same reason baseball pitchers bat last in baseball—they're normally weak hitters.

Why, you ask, so many bowlers in the lineup?

Because in cricket, substitutes are not allowed to bat or bowl. A captain, therefore, must carry in his lineup not only his "starting" bowlers, but any *change* (i.e., "relief") bowlers he thinks he'll need over the course of the entire match. Experience has shown that a team will normally need at least four, sometimes even five, specialized bowlers for any given match.

Inside the Batters Mind

"A great national game," Neville Cardus once said, "must draw out the whole man—not only his practical craftsmanship." Nowhere does cricket make greater demands on this totality of character than under the "sudden death" conditions its batters must live and work.

Without the redemptive prospect of a third, fourth or maybe fifth time at bat, the cricket batter can seldom afford to approach his batting with a single-minded "swing for the fences" baseball attitude.

He's got to have, instead, the mental dexterity to meet, without error, everything and anything that's thrown at him over a protracted period of time, trying to strike a workable balance between the always urgent imperative to make runs, with a sense of sheer survival.

In the span of a typical over, for example, a cricket batter may have to call up all his defensive skills to turn back a 90 mph, dead-on-wicket screamer, then shift gears and drive the next ball, an easier half-volley, to the boundary, then resist temptation and cautiously push away the next few pitches for a single here, another there, an unusual "pitty-pat" type of hitting to Americans only used to the all-out, full-blooded swings of their baseball batters.

Be rest assured the cricket batter, if he gets the right ball, can certainly hit it as hard and far as any home run king (C.I. Thornton's world record cricket hit of 504 feet, set way back in 1876, isn't about to take a back seat to any tape measure job in baseball), but this would only be a momentary power surge in his otherwise steady-minded push for those fifty, seventy-five, even hundred individual runs needed to put his team's score over the hump of reachability.

As he goes about his job the cricket batter does have, however, one advantage over his baseball counterpart—he'll always be working with a partner.

If he's having trouble with a particular bowler, for example, his partner, when the striker, can help him out by going only for an even number of runs during the over, a single on the final ball, so he (the partner) will always be facing the bowling as much as possible. As the non-striker, his partner can also help out by watching for byes, leg byes, or any other runs from hard-to-pick-up balls that may be hit backwards.

The Bowling "Attack"

Of course, the captain may lose the toss, in which case he's likely to have to start the match in the field, whether he wants to or not. The first thing he'll have to do in this situation is put together his bowling "attack," that is, decide who'll bowl, in what order, and for how long.

Odd as this may seem, these important decisions are pretty much planned around something as simple as the cricket ball's progressive wear and tear over the course of the innings.

When its new, the smooth and shiny cricket ball moves through the air and off the pitch with the least air resistance, a condition that can be used to best advantage by the team's fastest bowler, who, for that reason, almost always "opens" the bowling.

The fast bowlers objective is very simple: get the batters out, especially the opening batters, with sheer, overwhelming speed before they can settle in and find a rhythm. If the fast bowler can do this with a little deception or ball movement, all the better, but like a fastball pitcher in baseball, he's basically out to get the batters by virtue of his ability to simply beat bat with ball.

Even self-proclaimed cricket non-enthusiasts confess fascination with this spectacle of the fast bowler at work—the accelerating tension that builds, pace by pace, from his sprint-up, and sudden catharsis of a release so powerful its momentum will carry him half way down the pitch on the follow through. Reason enough why fast bowling has always been honored as one of cricket's more "glamorous" positions, invariably occupied by a team's most athletically gifted, competitively intense, if also frequently temperamental, players. The very best have always been a cricket batter's severest challenge, and certainly were the inspiration for the often heard cricket cliche, "batters may save matches, but bowlers win them."

But suppose the fast bowlers aren't having much luck getting anyone out, and don't seem as though they will once the batters get used to their style and pace.

Now may be a good time to bring on a medium pace bowler, who'll try to break the batters rhythm with some slower, "change of pace" type of deliveries.

The medium pacers usually bowl after the fast bowler because they can swing, or "curve," the cricket ball easier if its been scuffed up a bit, or, even better, if part of its surface is scuffed up while part of it is kept smooth, which the bowlers always try to do by constantly rubbing one side of it on their trousers when walking back to start their run up, one of cricket's more puzzling rituals for those who don't understand its purpose.

What the long reliever is to baseball, the medium pace bowler is to cricket; the staff "workhorse," who can be called on, especially if the fast bowlers need rest, or are "out of form," to perform yeoman duty keeping the scoring under control over long stretches with such steady, naggingly accurate, if not particularly overpowering, stuff, that one cricket writer's dubbed them "the meanest men in cricket."

After he's given his fast and medium pace bowlers some time, the captain may decide to exercise his third option and bring on a slow bowler.

As you might guess, the slow—also called a *spin*—bowler isn't out to beat anyone with speed or ball movement. He wants to, almost literally, "sneak" the ball past the batter with a variety of slow, spinning pitches that can be made to take, with a skillful flick of the fingers or roll of the wrist, devious and unpredictable bounces.

Looking at a slow bowler for the first time, most Americans usually can't help thinking how easy it should be to clobber a guy like this, who's throwing up his deliveries, off a diddly little two or three step run up, at about the same speed as a slow pitch softball pitcher.

This, of course, is exactly what the slow bowler would like to see every batter try, since the "spinner" knows that any attempt to knock the cover off of such an erratically bouncing ball will most likely just send it into the waiting hands of a nearby fielder as a mishit pop-up.

Experiences like this have taught even the most talented cricket batters to treat with extreme caution the slow bowler and his deceptively destructive array of pitches, "every ball a decoy, a spy sent down to get the lie of the land. Some balls easy, some difficult, and one of them—ah, which?—the master ball" (Neville Cardus).

This sequence of fast, followed by medium and then slow bowlers is the standard bowling attack. But the captain may also try to "customize" his attack to whichever batter happens to be up.

If the "scouting reports," for instance, say batter X is vulnerable to spin, that's what he'll usually get as soon as he comes up. Likewise the captain may try to cross up an over aggressive batter by bringing on a swing bowler, or try to take out the weak, bottom of the order batters with some straight-out fast bowling.

Field Placement
Through all this, of course, the bowlers aren't working alone.

They're backed up by ten other fielders, all very specifically and meticulously positioned in close conformity to the anticipated effects of each bowlers particular style.

When a fast bowler is on the job, for instance, two things are pretty likely to happen: (1) the batters, if they're smart, will try to play it safe and score most of their runs from cautious, shallow hits, and (2) even if they try to do this all the time, there's a good chance they'll still mishit a pitch sooner or later, either deflecting it backwards like a "foul tick," or, if they're trying to just block the pitch, hitting shallow pop-ups like the ones you see from a failed bunt attempt in baseball.

Fully expecting this, the fielders will normally play very shallow when their fast bowlers are operating, most within twenty yards of the batter, both in front of and behind him, close enough to prevent him from running on shallow hits, yet far enough to give themselves plenty of time to get their hands on any mishit balls (this is why the wicket-keeper, always strategically positioned far enough back from the batter to be able to snare any of these "foul ticks," doesn't need a face mask or chest protector).

From these positions, the fielders are, in effect, saying to the batter, "if you want to score runs, you're going to have to hit the ball hard enough to get it past us. But if you try and hit our fast bowler hard, sooner or later you're going to make a mistake, and when that happens, we're going to get you."

But maybe the batters aren't too cooperative about this and start to, in fact, send balls past the fielders. If this continues with any regularity, the captain may decide its time to re-deploy his fielders into a more strictly defensive arrangement.

Many of the fielders originally positioned behind the batter may now be moved around in front of him, or, if they're already playing there, be pushed back deeper into the outfield where they can cut off any boundary destined hits or get under the deeper fly balls. The captain may even move some players intentionally out of position, knowing the batter will have to take very risky swings to hit the ball through the gaps left in the field, or have his fielders chase balls at deceptive angles, hoping to cleverly run out some batter tempted into thinking he's got time to stretch out another run.

For the slow bowler, the captain may even deploy his fielders in something of a hybrid arrangement, positioning some, like those at the boundary, in fear of the worst (the bad pitch sent flying towards the stands), others, like those crouching cat-like right under the batter's nose, in hope of the best (the "master ball" that the batter, trying to block, only manages to gently pop up).

The wicket-keeper will also reposition himself for the slow bowler, moving up right next to the batter's wicket where he can more easily catch the slower pitches, and also watch to stump any batter tempted, in his frustration to hit the slow bowler, over the popping crease.

The Change Over

In addition to these purely tactical shifts, the fielders will also usually change their positions at the end of each over when the direction of the bowling is reversed.

If a fielder, for example, has been assigned a position behind the striker's wicket, he must, at the end of each over, then go down and take up the same position behind the opposite wicket. The fielders will usually continue to "flip flop" back and forth, this way—this shift is called a *change over*—after every over throughout the match.

In traditional multi-day cricket matches, a captain is completely free to place his fielders wherever he wants. This is usually not the case in limited overs matches, which usually require him to have at least five fielders, sometimes more, positioned within a sixty-yard circle laid out around the wickets for these kind of matches.

This rule was introduced into limited overs cricket to prevent captains from putting all their fielders deep in the outfield, a tactically correct strategy for these short type of matches, but one that, it was soon discovered, also made the game too defensive and unexciting for most fans.

The Declaration and Follow On

Aside from his purely tactical responsibilities, the cricket captain must also be, at least in the multi-day matches, something of a "time manager." He may be able to get his team into an insurmountable lead, but he won't win these extended matches unless he makes sure he's allotted himself enough time to get the other team out.

To help with this, the laws of the game provide him with a couple of valuable strategic options.

First, the captain doesn't have to bat until all his players are out. Anytime he thinks he's got enough runs to win, he can just stop batting, let the other team come up, and use the rest of the time trying to get them out (this is called a *declaration*).

Of course, by declaring, a captain runs the risk that the other team may beat his score in that time, so deciding just exactly when and under what circumstances to declare is often one of the most difficult judgments he has to make.

If his team's running up a big score in its first innings, he might not hesitate to declare, knowing that, even should the other team, in its first innings, score the same number of runs, he's still got another turn at bat.

But what if he's only got a modest second innings lead, with time running out? Should he keep batting, use up as much of the remaining time as possible and settle for a draw? Or should he go for the win, declare, and gamble he can get the other team out in the remaining time, before they can beat his score?

Much less complicated is the second tactical option, which allows the captain to switch the batting order at the end of the first innings if his team's ahead by a prescribed number of runs, usually between 150 and 200 if its a professional match.

This maneuver (called a *follow on*), can be a time saver because it forces the other team to make up its first innings deficit before it can field again.

For example, lets say Team A scores 300 runs in its first innings (a normal pro score), Team B 100 runs in its first innings. Already ahead by 200 runs, Team A, rather than bat right away, forces Team B to "follow on" and bat instead. Let's say Team B, in its second innings, does better and makes 275 runs, for a grand total of 375.

Now Team A, when it comes to bat, only has to make 76 runs to win. If Team A had not enforced the follow on (they don't have to) and had, instead, batting in regular order, they may have ended up scoring many more runs, and taken up much more time, than they needed to win.

What's more, if Team B, following on, had made anything less than 200 runs in its second innings, Team A would have won the match without even having to bat a second time. When this happens, a team is said to have won *by an innings*, which simply means the winning team scored more runs batting once, than their opponents did batting twice.

Chapter Three
The Umpires

A cricket match is officiated by two umpires, one at each wicket.

The umpire at the bowler's wicket normally stands about a yard behind the wicket, directly in line with, and looking down at, the strikers wicket.

Here he's in the best position for calling no balls, wides and for answering appeals for such types of outs as LBW, bowled, and caught, his primary umpiring duties. In addition, he's also responsible for starting and stopping play, counting the number of balls for each over, signalling fours and sixes, and for calling run out attempts at his wicket, which he usually has to do by moving off to the side of the wicket whenever the batters are running, much like a baseball umpire moving to the side for calls at home plate.

His partner, at the other wicket, is positioned in the outfield, about twenty yards straight out from the back of the striker in line with the popping crease.

The batters umpire (always called, for reasons we'll explain next chapter, the *square leg* umpire), is primarily responsible for answering appeals for run outs and stumpings at his wicket, though he's also expected to watch the bowler for any illegal arm motion.

Since the direction of the bowling reverses every six pitches, both umpires must alternate, at their respective wickets, between these two positions at the end of each over.

That is, the square leg umpire will move up behind his wicket and become the bowling umpire every over the fielding team bowls from his end. The bowlers umpire will likewise position himself in the outfield and become the square leg umpire during those overs when the batters at his end are hitting.

The two umpires continue to "flip flop" back and forth from these two positions after each over, throughout the match.

There are nine basic umpiring signals in cricket:

23

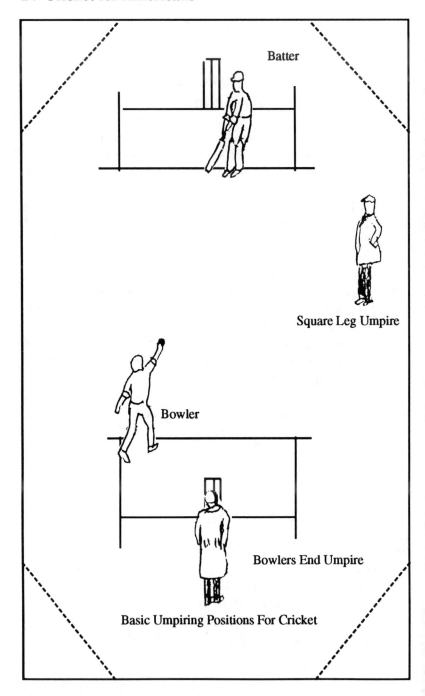

Batter

Square Leg Umpire

Bowler

Bowlers End Umpire

Basic Umpiring Positions For Cricket

A *six* is signified by raising both hands above the head, just like a "touchdown" signal in American football.

A *four*, is signaled by waving one arm from side to side across the chest.

A *short run* (where the batter misses the popping crease when running) is signaled by bending one arm up and touching the shoulder.

Out is signaled by raising the index finger.

Umpires signify a *no ball* by extending one arm straight out to the side, a *wide* by extending both arms out.

A *bye* is signaled by raising one arm above the head, a *leg bye* by raising one leg and touching the knee.

When a cricket umpire crosses his arms back and forth below his waist, he's signalling *dead ball, not* calling anyone "safe," for which there is, surprising as it may seem, no official cricket signal.

If a cricket umpire believes a batter is safe, he'll either just say "not out" or make no signal at all.

Although cricket umpires—whose official uniform consists of a white coat, tie, and dark trousers—are, like baseball umpires, delegated considerable authority (they are the sole judges of the fitness of grounds, fair and unfair play, among other things), they are not, officially, required to extend any decision except on appeal, a "let them play" arrangement quite different from a baseball umpire's highly intrusive (at least to a cricketer) obligation to make a theatrical call on every pitch and every hit. At all levels of play, the guiding principle for cricket umpiring has always been "he who does his job least noticeably, has done it best."

Most Americans would probably be very surprised to also know that cricket umpires have no real authority to remove, and very little to actually discipline, any player during an actual match. A cricket umpire can, for example, disbar a player he thinks is bowling dangerously from bowling for the rest of the innings, and is empowered to report disruptive incidents to authorities for post-match disciplinary measures, but he has no authority, and never had, to actually "kick" him, or any other player, out of the game.

The fact that there have been very few incidents in cricket history that have ever warranted such action is perhaps the strongest testimony to how deeply an unwritten, if sometimes over-romanticized, code of sportsmanship still pervades the game.

The Umpire's official signals.

Chapter Four
Cricketspeak

Consider the following, excerpted from the description of a typical cricket match:

Winterbottom yorked Miller for a duck and three balls later had Dawson caught behind five runs short of his century. Pope now joined Jensen and together, the two local boys were able, with some crisp driving between cover and mid-off, to put on 47 for the sixth wicket before the later lost his middle stump trying to pull Newton, now bowling his slow off-breaks around the wicket, over deep square leg.

All sound Greek to you?

That shouldn't be particularly surprising. Cricket, like baseball, is one of these sports that's, over the years, virtually invented its own private language.

No-one, however, should be intimidated by all these seemingly unintelligible terms, phrases and turns of expressions. Most of them are simply cricket's way of describing many of the same ball playing features you'd find in baseball—types of "pitches," batting style, fielding positions etc.

What's more, cricket terminology tends to be far more standardized than the ever-evolving, cliche-heavy language of baseball. Once you know, for example, that cricket's big hit is a "six," that's pretty much all you need to know. It doesn't go by any half dozen or so colorful but confusing aliases, "homer," "dinger," "gopher ball," etc., someone would also have to know with its baseball counterpart, the home run.

The Field: On and Off
You can get an idea of how this works with cricket's playing area, which has no right, center or left "fields." It's simply divided

into two equal halves by an imaginary line running straight down the middle of the pitch. The right half of the ground (from the striking batters angle) is called the *off* side, the left half the *on*, or interchangeable, the *leg* side.

As you'll see, many features of the game derive their names from, or can be understood in relation to, this division, i.e., the pole of the wicket farthest from the batter is always called the *off stump*, the one closest to him the *leg stump* (the middle pole is just that, the *center stump*).

Pitches: The Sticky and the Dead

We've already seen how important the condition of the pitch can be to planning match strategy. For that reason, specific names have actually been assigned to pitches of varying conditions.

A *dead* pitch, for example, is one that's dry and firm, but a little soft, just the kind a captain would want to bat on because the ball tends to bounce low, even, and a little slow.

A *lively* or *fiery* pitch, one that's hard and very dry, on the other hand, is just what a captain would want for his fast bowlers because the ball tends to "kick," i.e., come off the pitch with a high, difficult-to-hit bounce.

The slow bowler prefers to have either a *turning* pitch, one into which his spinning balls can "bite," or, best of all, a notorious *sticky wicket*, which really doesn't have anything to do with the wickets at all, but is a pitch whose damp and drying surface induces almost unplayably erratic bounces.

For all its notoriety, the sticky wicket has pretty much become a thing of the past, at least in professional cricket, where all pitches are now routinely covered with a tarp to keep them from getting wet.

The Bowlers: Swingers, Cutters and Googlies

The bowler, as we would expect, is preoccupied with only one thing: getting batters out, and getting them out for as few runs as possible. So everything about him is described in terms of how, with what, and in which way he's going to do this.

Normally, he'll always try to *attack the off stump* (keep the ball slightly "outside"), trying to maintain *a good line and length*

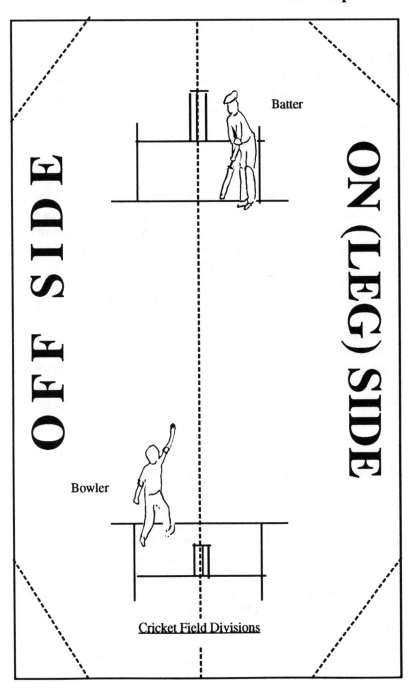

Cricket Field Divisions

(bounce the ball at the wicket, but not too close to the batter), so that, if he can't get the batter out, he'll at least be able to *tie him down* (keep the batter from scoring), or maybe even bowl a *maiden* (an over in which no run is scored off the bat).

If he's a *pace man*, or a *quickie* (fast bowler), he might try to surprise the batter with an occasional *in swinger* or *out swinger* (pitches that, respectively, curve into or away from the batter), a low *yorker* (one that bounces behind the popping crease), or even a *bouncer* (one that bounces up at the batter head high, cricket's "brush back" pitch.

He'll usually try to avoid bowling *short* (bounce the ball so far from the batter that it results in a high, easy-to-hit *long hop*), as well as *over pitching* the ball (bouncing it so close to the batter that he'll have an easy-to-hit half volley). And he definitely wants to stay away from any *full tosses*, pitches that reach the batter on the fly, the easiest of all to hit.

The medium pace bowler might bowl an *off* or *leg cutter*, pitches whose clockwise and counter-clockwise spin will make them sharply bounce, respectively, into or away from the batter. The slow bowler applies this same principle to his slower *leg* and *off breaks*, which he may also try to *flight* (throw at different heights). The slow bowler may even try to bowl cricket's most difficult pitch, the well-known *googly*, which is really nothing but an off break bowled with a motion to make the batter think it's a leg break.

All types of bowlers may try to vary the angle of their deliveries by sometimes bowling *over the wicket* (on the left side of the wicket, if he's a righty), sometimes *around the wicket* (on its right side).

All these different types of deliveries are thrown with one objective in mind; to get one of them past the batter and *clean* or *comprehensively* bowl him, to *spread eagle* his stumps.

But the bowler would also be quite happy to see the batter *caught behind* off a *thin edge* (the wicket-keeper catches the batter's "foul tick"), *caught in the deep* from a long fly ball, *caught and bowled* (where the bowler himself makes the catch) or even have him *trapped* (out LBW).

If the bowler can get the batter out any of these ways he's

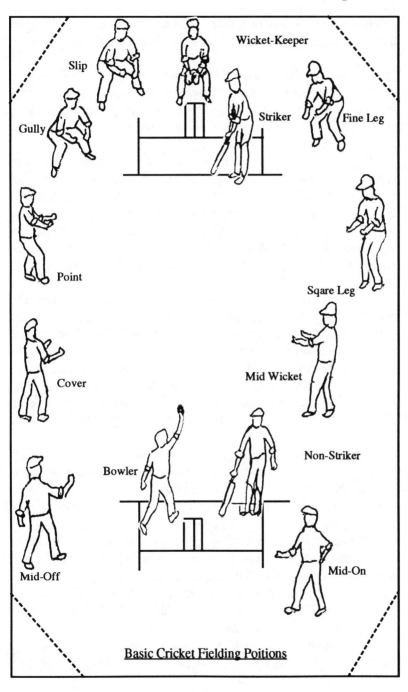

Basic Cricket Fielding Poitions

taken a wicket, and if he's lucky enough to take three wickets on
three successive balls, he's got himself a much coveted *hat trick.*

Batting: Sweeps, Hooks and Pulls

The batter, of course, will be operating in terms of the proper
mind set and technique to counter all this, trying to score as many
runs off the bowler as possible while minimizing, as much as he
can, all risks of getting out.

Until he *gets his eye in* (gets used to the pitch and the bowlers
style) he'll usually play with a *straight bat* (swing with safe, high
percentage, vertical strokes), trying to deflect some pitches
backwards with a careful *leg glance,* while pushing others away
with a cautious *check swing.* At other times he'll just block pitches
with a *forward* or *backward* defensive stroke,or maybe even
stonewall for a while (repeatedly block pitches without trying to
score).

Only after he's *played himself in* (warmed up) will he begin to
hit out (play more aggressively), by banging over-pitched
deliveries straight away with sharp *off* or *on drives,* short-pitched
balls with horizontal, baseball-like *cross bat* strokes. Swinging this
way, he'll *square cut* high bouncing pitches coming in outside his
off stump sharply to his right, *pull* the same type of pitches coming
in at his leg stump sharply to his left, or maybe, with a huge,
swooping *hook,* smash a bouncer or long hop so deep to his left
it'll end up in the stands.

Against a spin bowler he might drop down on one knee and try
to *sweep* the slowly bouncing ball around to his left, turn his hands
over and try to *reverse sweep* it the other way, or even *come out* to
the ball (go over the popping crease towards it) and try to *straight
drive* it right over the bowler's head.

If he's a batter who's *strong all around the wicket* (can hit to
all fields with power), has played a *solid innings,* and hasn't *given
a chance* (hit anything the fielders could catch), he might even
make a *century* (score a hundred runs), or, if he happens to be one
of the openers, might even *carry his bat* (outlast all his partners
until he's the last "not out" batter).

On the other hand, if he's not a *recognized batsman* (on the
team for his batting ability), and can't do anything except *slog*

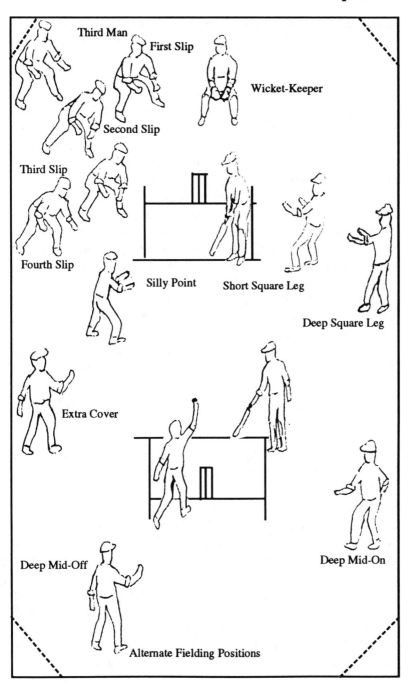

Third Man

First Slip

Wicket-Keeper

Second Slip

Third Slip

Fourth Slip

Silly Point

Short Square Leg

Deep Square Leg

Extra Cover

Deep Mid-Off

Deep Mid-On

Alternate Fielding Positions

(swing hard but indiscriminately), he'll probably end up *throwing his wicket away* (get himself out in a foolish way) for a *duck* (a score of 0).

Fielding: Points, Slips, and Covers

Cricket, like baseball, fielding can be largely described in terms of location and specialized function. If we start out from the wicket-keeper (this is with a right handed batter) and work around the field counterclockwise, the first person we'll run into is *slip,* crouched and alert behind the batter's wicket, ready to snap up any thin edges the batter might send his way, just as, a few yards to his right, *gully* stands ready to grab any *thick edges* (well hit "fouls").

Covering the off side in front of the wicket are, respectively, *point, cover* and *mid-off,* all poised and ready, about five to ten yards apart from each other, fifteen to twenty yards from the batter, to stop any balls from *piercing* (getting past) their side of the field.

Likewise the three fielders over in front of the batter, on the leg side, *mid-on, mid-wicket* and cricket's "hot corner," *square leg,* are, respectively, positioned to stop the batter from *making any scoring strokes* on their side of the field (now you also know why the umpire at the batters wicket, who stands near the square leg fielder, is called the "square leg umpire ").

A little further to the right of square leg, situated behind the batter, looking to cut off any glancing shots, is the final fielder, *fine leg.*

These are the basic cricket fielding positions, but players can be shifted to many other positions to accommodate different types of bowlers or to defend against certain types of batters.

Rather than have fielders at mid-wicket, mid-on or cover, for instance, a captain may prefer to have, for his fastest bowlers, especially if they can swing the ball away from the batter, a *second, third,* or even a *fourth slip,* positioned in an arch behind the batter ready to grab the thin edges likely to result from this type of bowling.

He may also put, fifteen to twenty yards behind the slip fielders, someone at *third man* to catch deep "foul balls," or move fielders in from their normal depth at square leg and point right up next to the batter, creating, respectively, *short square leg* and that much parodied, but very demanding position, *silly point.*

If the batters seem to be piercing his off side with too much regularity, the captain may fill the gap between cover and point with an *extra cover.* Too much heavy hitting towards the on side, or down the middle, may force him to move mid-off, mid-on or square leg deeper, making these fielders, respectively, *deep mid-off, deep mid-on* and *deep square leg.*

A captain who wants to shift any of his fielders, wherever they are, a little to the right or left of where they're positioned, can have them either play *finer* (move more parallel to the line of the pitch) or *squarer* (at more of a right angle to the line of the pitch).

Following the Game: Winning and Losing by Wickets

The ebb and flow of actual play—the falling-behinds, catching-ups, staying-withs—as dramatically common in cricket, as in any other sport, can be conveniently followed on the basis of each team's ten outs, or *wickets* as they're called in this context.

A team that starts its innings needing 200 runs to win, for example, may quickly *lose its first four wickets* (see its first four batters be put out) and find itself *63 for 4* (its got 63 total runs with four of its batters out). But then batter Jones may come in *with four wickets down* and, with his partner, *put on 87 for the fifth wicket* (score, between them, 87 runs after there's been four outs) and boost his team's score, by the time he's out, up to *150 for 5.* After that, the team may *lose its next three wickets for 25* (its next three batters get out for a combined 25 runs) and so end the day *with two wickets in hand* (two batters yet to be put out) and a score of *175 for 8.* The next day the team might then manage to reach run #200 *without further loss of wicket* (no more batters put out) and so win the match *by two wickets* (they've beaten the other team's score with two outs to spare).

This, in fact, is how all final scores are given, by wickets, for matches won by the team batting second. If a team, for example, has beaten the other team's score with five outs to spare, it's *won by five wickets*; with six outs to spare, its *won by six wickets* etc.

The Action Itself: Collapsing, Punishing, Recovering

As a game who's highest imperative is to maintain good form over an extended period, cricket's always been expressed in terms of clinical variation, rather than hyperbolic excitement.

You're seldom going to come across any impassioned sports reports of "red hot" cricket batters "killing the bowling" or "going into slumps." At their best, cricket batters only *play the ball well*, or respectfully *punish* the bowlers, and, in the worst of times only suffer a *loss of form*.

Likewise you're not likely to find any descriptions of "overpowering" fast bowlers, throwing with their "good stuff," only talk about those who are *penetrating*, capable of an occasional *inspired spell*. A baseball pitcher who "can't find the strike zone" is out and out "wild." The bowler who *loses his line and length* discreetly becomes *expensive*.

So the cricket fielder who snares, one handed, a hot liner hasn't made a "terrific play," he's just had the unhappy batter *well caught*. Should this same fielder miss a ball, he hasn't "muffed," or "booted" it, he's inadvertently *let the batter off* with a *dropped catch*, and certainly hasn't committed any "error," because there's no such statistical category in cricket.

Should a cricket team's batters go down like duck pins, they haven't been "blown away," they've only suffered a *collapse*. And if they manage to turn things around next innings, they haven't "come roaring back," they've only *recovered*.

Now that we've cracked the "secret" code of cricket terminology, lets go back to that passage at the beginning of the chapter. How would you "translate" it?

How about this:

Winterbottom bowled Miller, who hadn't made a run, with a pitch that bounced behind his popping crease, and, three pitches later, got out Dawson, who had made 95 runs, when the wicket-keeper caught his "foul tick." With five batters now out, Pope came up to bat and with his partner, Jensen, scored, between them, 47 runs, mostly by hitting the ball to the right side. Then Jensen tried to hit a slow, clockwise spinning ball from Newton—who was bowling from the right side of the wicket—deep to his left, missed it, and was bowled when the ball hit the center pole of his wicket.

Elementary my dear Watson! Elementary!

Chapter Five
How to Read Cricket Statistics

If you're one of these people who likes to play around with sports statistics, then cricket's certainly your kind of game.

Like baseball, cricket seems to be one of these sports that naturally lends itself to an almost limitless variety of measurement, quantification and numerical analysis.

Turn to the sports pages of just about any local newspaper in a cricket playing country and you'll find, during the cricket season, everything from how many wides bowler X threw in yesterday's match, to how many runs his team had at the fall of its third wicket, to who's currently on top of the season batting averages.

The Scorecard

The most important statistical vehicle for all this information is the cricket scorecard, which, despite its outwardly different appearance, pretty much serves the same purpose as a standard baseball boxscore; it simply summarizes who scored what, when, how, and who got out who, when and how.

The standard cricket scorecard (see Figure 1) is divided into four sections: the heading, followed by a batting, team scoring and bowling analysis.

The heading (1) is more or less the "vital information" section of the scorecard. It gives you things like team names, match location, winner of the toss, result, and *Man of the match* (i.e., MVP) recipient.

Figure 1

1	*WESSEX VS ANGLIA*	Played at: Linton Oval
	Date: June 1, 1991	Toss won by: Wessex
	Result: Wessex won by 42 runs	Man of the Match: I.A. Jones

2 Wessex	3		4 Anglia		
I.A. Jones	c Daft bNewton	117	*E.Wilson	c King b Woods	29
T.A. Smith	b McDonald	27	J.Henry	b Long	37
*M. Hampton	c & b McDonald	52	M. Schwartz	c Barry b Long	7
J. McDermott	st Haines b Murphy	0	S.Burns	lbw Woods	27
P.E. Barry	lbw Newton	37	L.Smith	c Hampton b Long	71
S. Johnson	c(sub) b Murphy	14	K.Daft	run out	0
†D. King	run out	2	†H.Haines	b Hicks	2
J. Hicks	b Newton	9	N.Lindwood	c Jones b Woods	27
W. Brown	not out	2	Murphy	b Brown	12
L.A. Long	b Newton	0	G.McDonald	not out	4
C. Woods	b Murphy	0	J.Newton	b Long	0
6 B 3 lb 2 w 1, nb 2		8	B 4 lb 6		10
	Total	268	5	Total	226

7 Fall of Wickets: 1-57, 2-179,3-181, 4-229, 5-241, 6-252, 7-258, 8-267 9-268, 10-268

Fall of Wickets: 1-59, 2- 70, 3-90, 4-161, 5-163, 6-171, 7-203, 8-218 9-223, 10-226

8 Anglia Bowling	O	M	R	W	Wd	Nb	Wessex Bowling	O	M	R	W	Wd	Nb
Newton	18	1	83	4	1		Woods	16	0	69	3		
McDonald	15	1	70	2	1		Long	14	1	4	4		
Murphy	13	0	62	3			Brown	12	1	54	1		
Lindwood	9	0	45	0			Hicks	11	0	5	1		

Immediately below the heading are the team batting summaries, each broken down into three columns.

The first column (2) lists the names of each batter in the order that they came to bat. The captain's name is always preceeded by an asterisk (*), the wicket-keeper's by a dagger (†).

The second column (3) tells you how each batter was put out, by which fielder, if any, and who was bowling at the time the batter was put out.

In our sample scorecard, we can see that Jones, Wessex's first batter, was caught ("c") by the Anglian fielder Daft, when Newton was bowling ("b"). The number two batter, Smith, was bowled ("b") by McDonald, who also caught, while bowling ("c & b") the next batter, Hampton.

Batter number four, McDermott, was stumped ("st") by Haines, the Anglian wicket-keeper, with Murphy bowling, while Barry, number five, was out leg before wicket ("lbw") with Newton bowling. The next batter, Johnson, was caught by a substitute fielder ("sub") while King, number seven, was run out. The name of the bowler's not given on a run out because he's not credited with taking a wicket with this type of out.

The number nine batter, Brown, is listed as "not out" because he was the batter left over after everyone else on his team had been put out.

The number of runs each batter scored is recorded in the third column (4), at the bottom of which (5) is the team's total score, always the sum of the runs scored by the batters plus any "extras" (6), i.e., byes, leg byes, no balls and wides.

On our scorecard, we see that of Wessex's 268 total runs, eight were extras; 3 byes ("B") , 2 leg byes ("lb") , one wide ("w") , and 2 no balls ("nb") .

Extras are always tabulated separately like this because, not being runs scored from a hit ball, they can't be credited to any batter.

The third section of the scorecard, "Fall of Wickets" (7), gives the team's score at the time each of its ten outs was made.

Looking at your example, we can see that Wessex had made 57 runs by the time its first batter was put out; 179 by the time its second batter was out; 181 at the time its third batter was out, etc.

Breaking a cricket team's score down this way serves pretty much the same purpose as an inning-by-inning scoring breakdown in a baseball box; it provides a handy tool for comparing each team's scoring progress.

Again going back to our example, you'll notice that Anglia was actually doing a little better than Wessex at the fall of their respective first wickets, 59 to 57. At the fall of their second wickets, however, Anglia had only 70 runs, Wessex 179. At the fourth wicket, Anglia had some 60 runs less than Wessex, at the sixth wicket, almost 80 runs less.

Clearly, anyone scanning the fall of wickets section of this scorecard would immediately see that Anglia had been struggling to keep up with Wessex's scoring rate for most of the match.

Immediately below the "Fall of Wickets" is the last section of the scorecard, the bowling analysis (8).

This section, the equivalent of the pitching summary in a baseball box, breaks down each teams bowling performance into seven statistical columns.

The first column lists all the players on the team who bowled, in the order that they first came on to bowl.

The total number of overs each bowled is listed in the second column (under "0"), those of which were maidens in the third (under "M"). The fourth column (under "R"), tells you how many runs each bowler gave up, the fifth (under "W"), how many wickets each took. The last two columns list, respectively, the number of wides ("Wd") and no balls ("Nb") each bowler threw, if any.

Some scorecards will condense each players bowling analysis into just four numbers, which would then indicate, respectively, the number of overs bowled, maidens, runs allowed and wickets taken. If Newton's bowling analysis were given this way, for example, it would read 18-1-83-4.

Individual Statistics

The scorecard, of course, only gives you figures for a single match.

If you want to know how a particular player has been doing, over an extended period of time, you have to look up his individual statistics.

Let's say you want to know how the Wessex opener, I.A. Jones, has been doing this season and come across the following information about him:

	M	I	NO	HS	Runs	Ave
I.A. Jones	10	16	2	119*	490	35.0

What does this tell us about Mr. Jones?

The first three columns will tell you, respectively, how many two innings matches ("M") he's played in, how many innings ("I") he's played (been at bat), and how many of these at bats he was not out ("NO") .

The fact that Jones batted only sixteen times, in ten two-innings matches, rather than the expected twenty, immediately tells you that some of these matches were drawn, declared, or otherwise ended before he got to bat a second time.

The fourth column ("HS") gives you his highest individual score of the season (an asterisk by the score tells you he made it without being putout), followed by the total number of runs ("Runs") he's made.

His batting average listed in the final column ("Ave") is arrived at by dividing his total runs by the number of innings he's played *less* his "not outs," which, like walks in baseball, do not count as official times at bat.

If you're interested in knowing how a particular bowler's doing—let's say Anglia's J. Newton—you'll find his statistics broken down this way:

	0	M	Runs	W	Ave	5wi	B-B
J. Newton	211	19	840	42	20.0	3	7-89

Here the first two columns will tell you, respectively, how many overs he's bowled ("O"), and how many of these were maidens ("M"). The third column tells you how many runs ("Runs") he's given up, the fourth how many wickets ("W") he's taken. His average ("Ave"), column five, is arrived at by simply dividing the number of runs he's given up by the number of wickets he's taken.

Column six ("5wi") tells you in how many matches he's taken at least five wickets, if any, (anytime a bowler can take this many wickets in a match, he's done a good job) while the last gives you his best bowling performance ("B-B") of the season, which, in this case, was some match in which Newton took seven wickets while giving up 89 runs.

Both these hypothetical bowling and batting averages are quite normal for first-class cricket.

A professional cricketer who's on a team for his batting can normally be expected to average between 25 and 50 runs per match. If he can push this average above 60, he'll usually be in the running for the league batting crown.

Any first-class bowler who's giving up twenty runs or less per wicket over the course of a season, would be among the league leaders in this category.

Chapter Six
How to Watch a Cricket Match

If you're like most Americans, chances are pretty good that you'll get your first exposure to cricket by watching it.

It could be anything from a weekend parks game you happen to stumble on while strolling around London, to a pickup game you've spotted on a beach in Barbados, to an important test match you've been invited to attend by some friends in Sydney.

Whatever the level of play, a cricket match can be one of the most attractive forms of entertainment, but, like every other kind of sports event, the more you know about it, the more you're likely to enjoy what you see.

To give you an idea of what to expect at your first cricket match, we'll spend this chapter going through a hypothetical English professional match, from start to finish, exactly as you could expect to find it if you attended in person.

The first order of business is to decide which type of match we want to see.

Like most Americans, we're probably not used to sitting through anything longer than a two-or three-hour football or baseball game, so it'd probably be best to start out with one of the limited overs "Sunday League" matches.

These, the shortest of all first-class English cricket matches (only 40 overs per side), are still longer than a typical baseball game, but we know they'll be finished in only a single afternoon's worth of play.

Checking the papers, we see that Surrey, one of London's two professional clubs, will be playing its next Sunday League match at home against the Derbyshire County Cricket Club. We mark our calender and begin to count the days down.

Match day arrives overcast and drizzly, so we decide to call the Surrey grounds and inquire about "prospects of play," a service offered by most English clubs to let spectators know if the start of the match is expected to be delayed. No, we're told, the match is scheduled to start on time, and, in fact, the weather clears up quite nicely by the time we make our way to the subway and catch a train to South London's Kennington Oval, Surrey's home ground, which we have no trouble finding since it has its own stop marked on the subway system.

We pick up our ticket and program at the South Entrance, the famous "Hobbs Gate," named after Jack Hobbs, a famous Surrey player of the twenties, and settle into a comfortable ground level seat in the Laker Stand (named after, naturally, another famous Surrey player) just to the right of the club's stately old pavilion, which doubles as both its administrative center and its team changing quarters (cricket grounds have no "dugouts").

From here we're looking down the length of the pitch at about a thirty-five-degree angle, the preferred location for watching a match because we can see the batters and bowlers playing front on. If we've come early enough we might still find the teams at batting practice, or "net practice" as its called in cricket, because collapsible nets rather than movable cages are used. Or we might catch a glimpse of the grounds crew out touching things up, or the opposing captains tossing for innings, which they do alone, unsupervised by any umpires.

Otherwise we might spend the few minutes before start of play browsing through the match program, familiarizing ourselves with team rosters, and standings. Here we learn that we'll be watching the tenth match of the Sunday League, a single, round-robin competition, played between the seventeen county (professional) English cricket clubs,.

Surrey, coming into the match at 5-4, seems to be pretty much out of contention, but they can still play spoilers for Derbyshire, which, at 7-2 is very much in the running for league honors.

Looking over the individual player averages, we don't see anyone, on either team, who's among the league leaders in batting or bowling, though we're told by a resident expert in the next row, to keep our eye on Surrey's first year fast bowler from India who's been playing outstanding cricket for them all summer.

But now the match is about to start. We know this as soon as we see the umpires emerge from the pavilion and slowly begin to head down the clubhouse steps. In a moment they're through the small swinging gate at its foot and making their way out to the pitch where they set to work carefully setting the bails on the stumps, official notice that the match is now in progress.

The Derbyshire fielders are right behind them, ambling in single file down the same steps, out onto the field, where their captain sets to work assigning them to their respective positions, while his opening bowler, who gives his cap and sweater to the bowler's end umpire to hold while he'll be bowling, stretches out or takes a few warm-up tosses to the side of the pitch (the laws expressly forbid any practice on the game pitch itself).

A minute later the Surrey openers emerge from the pavilion, in their chocolate trimmed sweaters, embroidered with the Prince of Wales Feathers, and begin to make their way, accompanied by a warm round of applause, out to the pitch, passing the few seconds before they reach the center exchanging last minute ideas on how they'll play the bowling or start the innings.

Once at the crease, the striker immediately sets to work with many of the same type of ritualistic preparations we're used to seeing in baseball—scratching out a foothold in the turf, taking guard, fidgeting with equipment and helmet, going through a few practice swings etc.

When he's finally finished with all this, he takes one last sweeping glance around the field to make sure he knows where the fielders are positioned, steps to the crease, pats his bat to the turf, looks up, and rivets his eyes on the bowler, poised and ready, fifteen yards behind the opposite wicket, to start his run up.

"Play," the bowler's end umpire calls.

The bowler starts to sprint in, signal for the mid depth fielders to also start walking in towards the batter (which they do, each delivery, to get a jump on shallow hits) and for the wicket-keeper and close fielders to go into their cat-like crouch (so they're ready for any quick-reaction catches). His first ball's fast and straight, but it's outside the off stump and is allowed to go past without a swing. As he walks back to start his next run up, the ball's relayed back to him from wicket keeper to slip to point.

The next ball is also just outside the off stump, but its slightly overpitched and the batter has no trouble pushing it towards point for a check swing single, which he also does with the third and last balls of the over. The first boundary, a straight drive that beats a shallowish mid off, comes up the next over, two more in the third.

With some forty runs on the board in only the first half-hour, you're beginning to think the Surrey openers must already have the Derby bowlers figured out, until, that is, batter number two, a few pitches later, misjudges one and sees his off stump completely knocked out of the ground to a chorus of cheers from the Derby fielders. This is immediately followed by a round of hugs and high fives, a cricket ritual, you soon realize, that routinely follows the fall of every wicket.

Score: 44 runs for one wicket.

At the end of the over, the Derby captain decides to bring on a new bowler, a medium pacer, who immediately sets to work rearranging some of the fielders, a time the batters use, as they do during all bowling changes, huddling in the center of the pitch, comparing notes on what to expect from the new bowler.

After a few wary strokes, the batters see there's nothing particularly dangerous about this new guy, and soon have the runs coming again, until, just past 70, you suddenly hear another chorus of shouts and see the wicket keeper cheerfully tossing what seemed to be a missed ball high in the air. At first you're not sure what happened, but then you understand; Surrey's other opener's just been caught behind off a barely audible thin edge.

Score: 72 for 2.

Surrey's third wicket partnership now settles in and continues to move the score steadily along, up just past the century mark when another chorus of shouts, this one even louder than the ones before, rises from the field. No one's caught the ball, and the wicket's not broken, so you conclude, correctly, that the batter, who's dejectedly making his way back to the pavilion, helmet off, bat tucked under his arm, has just been given out LBW.

Score now: 103 for 3.

You're particularly anxious to see the next Surrey batter, a West Indian, because you've heard he's supposed to be one of the team's big hitters.

You don't have to wait very long to see how he got this reputation.

In his very first over he sends a couple of balls to the boundary past cover, another to deep mid-wicket for three, all played with more "athletic" looking strokes than you've seen with the other Surrey batters. Another one of his searing grounders, which even a deeply placed Derby fielder, diving full-length, like a basketball player trying to keep the ball in bounds, can't stop, reaches the boundary next over, two more in the over after that.

Its all very entertaining cricket, but it's also a little too "loose" even for a limited overs match, so we're really not that surprised to see him clean bowled, an over or two later, trying to add a six to his score.

Now at 154 for 4, and scoring about six runs an over, Surrey's not doing too badly, but with less than fifteen overs left, their number four, who up to this point has forty unspectacular runs to his credit, decides its time to start picking things up.

This, at least, is what you assume from the way he's now beginning to open his shoulders, trying to put more force behind his strokes. In a few minutes he's up to fifty runs, at which point play is momentarily stopped so he can acknowledge, by raising his bat overhead or tipping his cap, the crowds appreciative applause, an honor accorded, by custom, to all batters, friend or foe, when they reach a half or full century.

Then its back to work, but it isn't long before his partner, batter number six, trying to pull a ball over square leg, is caught in the deep by a nice running catch that would have warmed the heart of any baseball center fielder.

You see in your game program that the Surrey captain, who's coming up next, made almost 300 runs in a match earlier this season. But with only a few overs left, you soon understand he's more than happy to let his well-set partner do most of the batting.

With the Surrey total now well past 200, Derby has to bring back a slow off-break bowler (in this competition, no-one's allowed to bowl more than eight overs per match), but number four hits this guy just as hard, even sending one of his deliveries, disastrously short-pitched, into the stand over deep mid-wicket for the first six of the match (which one of the fans promptly throws back to the fielders—sorry, no souvenir balls in cricket).

By now everyone's anxious to see if he'll get a century, which, in fact, he does by cracking, appropriately enough, a straight drive, on the penultimate ball of the Surrey innings, all the way to the sight screen, a large rectangular, white panel set upright, in line with the wickets, just beyond the boundary so the batters can pick up the bowled ball from its background.

As the players head off the field to a warm round of applause, you see on the clubs mechanical, Wrigley Field-type scoreboard that Surrey's finished up with 248 runs for the loss of five wickets, a fairly decent score for this type of competition, but nothing, our neighbor sitting next to us says, Derby can't beat, with a little luck, on such a good batting pitch.

Derbyshire won't start their innings for another ten minutes (the maximum time allowed between innings), so you decide to get a bite to eat at the club catering services and spend a few minutes browsing around the club souvenir shop.

By the time you're back in your seat, Derby's already started their innings, batting, it strikes you, slower and more cautiously than Surrey did. You don't see much except a lot of check swings and quick singles, and, on one occasion, even a maiden over, an extremely rare event in limited overs cricket where a batting side can hardly afford to let six straight deliveries go by without a run. But it all seems to work well enough for the Derby openers, who inch their score along this way, past fifty, then seventy-five, even up towards one hundred.

Then, with the score right at 100, number one momentarily hesitates on his partner's call for another single and is run out with a crisp, direct hit on his stumps from cover.

This moment of excitement, however, quickly passes as Derby's second wicket partnership immediately resumes its inadventurous scoring rate, digging hard for runs, but not hitting with much power. By playing this way, our expert in the next row tells us, Derby's just trying to keep wickets in hand until they have to make an all-out rush for runs in the final few overs.

If so, the tactic seems to be working fairly well so far. Though scoring a good run less per over than Surrey did, the number two and three batters keep pushing the score relentlessly along, a run here, another there, through three Surrey bowling changes, innumerable fielding changes and adjustments, and at least three vociferous, but denied appeals for LBW, until its almost up to 200.

Then a moment of controversy.

With the score eight runs shy of a double century, Derby's second opener, who's been flirting with danger, it's seemed to you, for most of the innings with his aggressive running between the wickets, pushes one towards a shallow mid-wicket, takes off for another single, and dives head-first over the crease just as the ball crashes into his stumps.

From where you're sitting it seems the batter and ball arrived at the same time, but the umpire's index finger goes up almost immediately. The batter can't believe it, and, on his way back to the pavilion, lets everyone on the field know it by sending back a few choice remarks at the umpire.

To the Surrey captain, however, its not only the end of a long and troublesome partnership, it also signals time to bring on the Indian bowler you've been hearing so much about.

The fireworks begin almost as soon as the guy starts bowling.

His second delivery raps the pads of the incoming batter and immediately has him on the way back to the pavilion, LBW, for a duck. A no-ball later he swings a short one away from the newly arrived number five and also gets him for a duck when the ball catches the shoulder of his bat and goes straight to point.

The next batter, probably unnerved, you assume, with this sudden reversal of fortune, gets himself out on a suicidal run attempt almost as soon as he's up.

Even the long surviving number three, who's been patiently grafting most of his runs off the medium pacers, fails to adjust quickly enough to the Indian's surprising pace, and, an over later, is clean bowled. The next batter, number eight, does get a few runs off the rampaging Indian but he pushes his luck trying to off drive one slightly short of length and holes out to mid-off.

Even you can see that Derby's strategy, at this point, seems to have backfired. Their five expectant run makers have gone down for only some twenty runs, leaving the teams last three batters a scant five overs to make the 46 runs still needed to win.

Derby's last recognized batter, their wicket-keeper, manages to reduce this number by twenty before he's bowled, numbers nine and ten, though both bowlers with only single digit batting averages, reduce it by another half dozen with what could only be described as some hair raising running between the wickets. A high fly ball dropped by square leg gives them another run, a thick edge through a vacant slip position four more.

Then another moment of controversy.

Trying to pull a short one to leg, number nine sends a low liner to mid-wicket who, diving forward full-length, catches the ball just as it's about to touch the ground.

Or did he?

The bowling end umpire, who must make this call, isn't sure, so he decides to huddle with his partner at square leg. After a few suspenseful moments the verdict comes; out, caught.

As the last Derby batter makes his way to the crease the scoreboard tells you he and his partner still have to come up with fourteen runs and have only eight pitches to do it. If they just make thirteen, and tie Surrey, they'll still lose because in a limited overs match, a tie goes to the team with the fewer wickets lost (Surrey, you remember, only lost five wickets in its innings. Derby's already lost nine).

For the first time all afternoon, the atmosphere seems to be charged with something like the suspenseful tension you know so well from a close, late innings baseball game, especially in the way everyone moves under the same awful weight of an impending climax: the batter nervously fidgeting at the crease, preparing himself for the final do-or-die swings; his teammates anxiously watching from the Pavilion balcony; the Surrey captain frantically gesturing his players into last minute fielding adjustments.

Then the final act begins.

A few more nerve-wracking singles, followed by a fumbled overthrow gets Derby up to 240. But now there's only three pitches left, so number ten decides to try one of these go-for-broke, baseball like strokes you only see in limited overs cricket, and, swinging this way, actually manages to get hold of the next pitch and send it past cover for four. Another one of these and a scratch single can even now still win it for Derby.

But the Surrey bowler's seen this kind of batting ploy before. At least this is what you conclude, somewhat anti-climactically, as you see him, next pitch, cleverly bowl the over aggressive batter with a fast yorker to finally wrap things up for Surrey, and bring to an end your day "at the ballpark."

"So the game goes on; its genius fruitful and multiplying" (Neville Cardus).

Chapter Seven
How to Teach Cricket to Americans

"the whole game is a constant exercise of muscle in batting and running, and skill in bowling and catching the ball."

Harper's Weekly Oct 3, 1868

The old cliche, that some sports are meant to be played rather than watched, is probably more true of cricket than any other sport.

Americans may not be particularly interested in a sport they have to spend a couple of days watching, but once they've actually got a cricket bat in their hands, most would find it hard not to warm up to a game with such sky-high scores, simple rules and leisurely tempo, especially if they don't have to play it any longer than they want to.

For the benefit of those Americans interested in giving the game a try, this chapter will cover a basic beginners cricket program, that's been specifically designed for Americans who would like to start out on their own, or would like to introduce cricket to other Americans who have no prior knowledge of the game.

The step-by-step program—ideal for teachers or recreation instructors interested in cricket as a PE activity—will show, in eight, short, thirty-minute lessons, how to present a safe, "softball" type of cricket that's fully suitable for individuals of all ages and athletic abilities.

Equipment

If you're working with elementary age students, the minimum equipment you'll need are two size 4 cricket bats, a set of regulation (*not* junior) size wickets, and a rubber softball.

If you're working with junior high students, you should use

53

size 5 or 6 bats; with senior high students, size 6 or "Harrow" size bats. If you want to use wicket-keeping gloves (optional for elementary and junior high, but recommended for senior high classes) you should use adult, *not* junior size gloves. No protective pads or batting gloves will be needed for this program.

A list of cricket equipment suppliers can be found in chapter 11.

Playing Area

You can use just about any open, short-cropped grassy area for playing cricket, a football or soccer field, or the outfield of a softball diamond.

The playing area should be at least fifty yards in diameter for elementary grades, sixty yards for junior high, seventy yards for senior high. The entire playing area should also be bounded by either a chalk line, cones or marking flags. If you're playing on a football or soccer field, their sideline markings can serve as boundaries.

The wickets should be placed about fifteen yards apart for elementary grades, seventeen to eighteen yards apart for junior high. The wickets should only be placed at their regulation distance, twenty-two yards, for senior high students.

Creases

Mark the creases at their regulation lengths, i.e., the popping crease should not be less than four feet from the wicket, the return creases (optional for elementary and junior high grades) should be marked 8' 8" apart. No bowling crease need be marked.

Lesson One: Batting

(Note: If possible, the first four lessons should be held indoors. In these instances, creases can be marked with masking tape; chairs or marking cones can be used for wickets).

Objectives: In this lesson students will:
(1) Learn the names and functions of basic cricket equipment.

(2) Learn the names and functions of the markings and structures in the playing area.

(3) Learn the rules pertaining to cricket batting.

(4) Practice batting.

Set-Up: Set of wickets (or substitutes) with creases laid out in regulation configuration.

Equipment: Five cricket bats and tennis balls.

Unit Introduction:

The teacher may here want to introduce the unit by saying something like this: "Today boys and girls we'll begin our cricket unit. Cricket is one of the worlds great sports. It originated in England and is now widely played in almost every English-speaking country of the world. Like baseball, cricket's a bat and ball team sport. Teams alternate batting and fielding, trying to score runs when batting, trying to get batters out when fielding. Although most of you have probably never played or seen cricket before, I'm sure you'll all find the game as much fun as any other sport we've played."

Lesson: Here the teacher should cover the following points in this order:

*The cricket bat is called just that, a "bat," not, a "paddle." The ball is always hit on its flat side.

*Only one fielder is allowed to wear gloves in cricket, the wicket-keeper, who's just like a catcher in baseball. All other fielders must play barehanded.

*Cricket is played on a large, open grassy area. There are no bases, backstops or pitching mounds, only two sets of three wooden poles, called the wickets. They function something like bases in cricket and are, officially, 22 yards apart, together, 9" wide. The two pieces of molded wood resting in grooves on top of the wickets are called "bails."

*Four feet in front of each wicket is the game's most important marking. Its called the popping crease, and serves as the safe line for cricket. The two lines running back from the popping crease, called the return creases, mark out the area from which the "pitcher" (don't call him a bowler yet) must throw.

*The cricket batter stands in front of, and a little to the side of one wicket and tries to hit balls the "pitcher" throws from the other wicket.

*There's no "foul territory" in cricket; the batter can hit the ball anywhere.

*There's no balls or strikes in cricket.

*The "pitcher" can throw the ball on the bounce as well as on the fly. There's no penalty if he hits the batter with the ball.

*The batter's out if he lets a pitch hit his wicket and knock off at least one bail.

*The batter's out if he hits a ball a fielder catches on the fly.

*The batter's also out if he hits his own wicket, even accidentally, and knocks off at least one bail while batting.

*(Optional) The batter's out if he blocks a ball from hitting his wicket with his body, even accidentally.

(15 minutes)

Exercise: From here divide the class into as many groups as there are bats and arrange each group into batting, pitching and fielding positions as illustrated in Diagram #1.

Starting from this arrangement, have the pitchers lob the tennis balls, underarm, to the batters on one bounce,until each batter has had four hits. Then rotate every one in the groups up towards the batter. Continue rotating this way until everyone in each group has had a turn to bat, pitch, field and keep wicket.

(15 minutes)

Pointers: During this exercise, the teacher should stress the following points:

*Swing at everything, even pitches that are thrown at or behind you.

*Move to the ball. You don't have to stay in one place when batting in cricket.

*Don't worry if you miss the ball. There are no balls or strikes.

Question and Answer:

These are some of the more common questions the teacher may be asked during this lesson:

*Do you have to knock off both bails to get the batter out? (No)

*Do the batters have to stand behind the popping crease when batting? (No)

*Can the batters go over the popping crease to hit the ball? (Yes)

Diagram 1

*Can you hit the ball if it bounces more than once? (Yes)

Lesson Two: Scoring

Objectives: In this lesson students will: (1) Learn how runs are scored in cricket (2) learn how batters going for runs are put out (3) practice scoring runs and getting batters out.

Set-up and Equipment:
Three bats and a rubber softball. One set of wickets and creases in regulation configuration.

Lesson: Here the teacher should cover the following points in this order:

*Cricket batting is always done in pairs, one batter at each wicket.

*Batters don't have to run when they hit the ball.

*If they do run, they must carry their bats with them.

*A run is scored when both batters get safely over their opposite popping creases.

*Batters can keep running back and forth, as often as they think they can safely. They score another run each time they switch wickets.

*A fly ball hit out of the playing area scores six automatic runs.

*A ground ball hit out of the playing area scores four automatic runs.

*The batters can run if the wicket-keeper misses the ball.

*Fielders can get the batters out by hitting their wickets with the ball before they can get over their popping creases.

*There's no "double play" in cricket.

(8 minutes)

Exercise: Divide the class into two equal teams, one batting, one fielding. Two members of the batting team, with bats, assume normal batting positions at each wicket. Four members of the fielding team take up a "four corners" position around and about fifteen yards from the wickets, as per Diagram #2.

Starting from this position the teacher hits a "fungo" ball to one of the fielders. As soon as the ball is hit, the batters must run and try to score. The fielders try to get one of them out. If a batter is run out, another batter takes his/her place.

After the teacher has hit one "fungo" ball to each fielder, four new fielders and two new batters come up. Continue this way until everyone on the fielding team has fielded once and everyone on the batting team has batted once. Then have the two teams switch, and repeat. If you're using wicket-keeping gloves with your unit, you may add a fifth fielder, the wicket-keeper, covering the wicket.

(22 minutes)

Pointers: During this exercise the teacher should stress the following points:

*The batters can keep running on overthrows.

*Batters should always try to touch their bats down over the popping crease ahead of them.

*Fielders should be alert to "back up" all throws at the wicket.

Teacher

Diagram 2

Question and Answer:

These are some of the more common questions the teacher may be asked during this lesson:

*If I start to run and change my mind, can I come back to my wicket? (Yes)

*Am I out if I drop my bat? (No, just keep running, you can go back for it later).

*Can the batters "over run" the popping crease? (Yes)

*If you're a fielder and you see both batters have ended up at the same wicket, what do you do? (Hit the vacant wicket. The batter who ran from that wicket is now out).

*If I hit a ball and it goes down and hits the other wicket, is anyone out? (No, it's just a hit like any other hit. You can run if you want to).

*Is the ball dead if it hits the wicket? (Not unless someone is out).

*If the bails have been knocked off the wicket, how can I get anyone out? (Just hit the wicket without the bails).

Lesson Three: Bowling

Objectives: In this lesson, students will (1) learn the rules pertaining to "pitching," and (2) practice "pitching" in a game setting.

Set-up and Equipment:

Two pitches, set up in regulation configuration. Four bats, two tennis balls.

Lesson: Here the teacher should cover the following points in this order:

*The person who throws the ball to the batter in cricket is called a bowler.

*The bowler can take a run up to throw.

*He must keep his arm straight when throwing.

*He cannot go over the popping crease or outside the return creases until he releases the ball. Failure to do this, called a no ball, results in one penalty run for the batting team and the ball must be taken over.

*He must throw the ball within reach of the batter.

*Failure to do this, called a wide, also results in one penalty run for the batting team and the pitch must be taken over.

*The direction of the bowling is reversed every six pitches. This is called an over.

*Although the bowler can throw either overarm or underarm, everyone must bowl underarm during this program.

(7 minutes)

Exercise: Divide the class into four teams, two to a pitch. Two teams bat the other two field. The batting teams bat through their entire order and try to score runs, but no batter can bat for more than three pitches. Each person on the fielding teams bowls one over in rotation, bowling, however, in only one direction. When everyone on the batting team's had a turn to bat, the teams switch.

(23 minutes)

Pointers: During this exercise the teacher should stress the following points:

* Aim at the wicket. That's all you're trying to hit.

* Try to bowl the ball on one, low, fast bounce.

* Try to bounce the ball a few feet in front of the batter.

* Don't roll the ball.

Question and Answer:

These are some of the more common questions the teacher may be asked during this lesson:

* Can I change bowlers in the middle of an over? (Not unless the bowler's injured).

* Can I throw the ball on more than one bounce? (Legally, yes, but this is an easy ball to hit).

* Can I "fake" a pitch to try and catch the batter at my wicket over the popping crease? (Yes)

Lesson Four: Game Structure

Objectives: In this lesson students will (1) learn how a cricket match is structured, and (2) play a full scrimmage.

Set-up and Equipment:

Regulation pitch. Two bats, rubber softball, wicket-keeping gloves (optional).

Lesson: Here the teacher should cover the following points in this order:

*Officially, there's eleven players on a cricket team.

*A cricket match is played over one, or, at the most, two innings.

*An innings in cricket is completed when everyone on the batting team has come to bat and been put out, one after another.

*The very last batter does not have to be put out.

*When the batting team has been put out, the fielding team comes up and bats through their entire order.

*Whichever team has the most runs is the winner.

(5 minutes)

Exercise: Divide the class into two equal teams. Have them play a full scrimmage following these "house" rules:
(1) The batting order must alternate boy/girl,
(2) No batter can bat more than five pitches (teachers may modify this number depending upon class size).
(3) Everyone on the fielding team must bowl one over in rotation,
(4) Time permitting, play two innings.

(25 minutes)

Pointers: During the scrimmage, the teacher should stress the following points:

*Batters must always return to their original wickets after hitting a four or a six.

*The fielding team should position itself so that all areas of the field are covered.

*If the bowler is bowling from one side of the

wicket, the non-striker should always stand at the other side.

Question and Answer:

These are some of the more common questions the teacher may be asked during this lesson:

* Can I "pinch hit" for someone in cricket (No, but you can run for them if they can't run themselves)

* What if I can't continue batting? (You can come out and go back in later)

* Can I switch around the batting order during the game? (Yes)

Lessons Five through Seven: Organized Matches

Spend these sessions playing full matches following the same house rules from lesson four.

During these matches the teacher should continue to closely monitor and correct any errors in technique or misunderstandings about the rules. When working with elementary level students, the teacher may also want to assume responsibility for delegating bowling and wicket-keeping changes and for monitoring each batters time at bat.

To further heighten interest in these matches, the teacher may want to:

* Divide the class into four permanent teams and play a three game round-robin tournament.

* Assign the names of cricket-playing countries to each team (i.e., England, Australia etc.).

* Show video tapes of professional cricket if the weather does not permit outdoor play.

* Have students research cricket at their school or local library and submit a written report.

Lesson Eight: Evaluation (optional)

Junior/Senior high teachers who would like to finish the unit with some kind of evaluation can do this by administering the following written examination (see Diagram #3).

The test, which can normally be completed in fifteen minutes or less, consists of twenty multiple-choice/true-false questions on basic rules, terms and game situations covered in the program.

Elementary level teachers who would like to evaluate their students skill development, can use the second test, designed to measure basic striking/throwing proficiency in the areas of batting, bowling, fielding and wicket-keeping.

Diagram 3

Multiple choice. Circle the correct answer.

1. Officially, how many players are on a cricket team?

(a) 8 (b) 9 (c) 10 (d) 11

2. The official distance between the wickets is:

(a) 17 yards (b) 20 yards (c) 22 yards (d) 25 yards

3. The player in cricket who functions like a pitcher in baseball is called a

(a) fielder (b) catcher (c) bowler (d) wicket-keeper

4. The only fielder in cricket who is allowed to wear gloves is called the

(a) wicket-keeper (b) bowler (c) outfielder (d) pitcher

5. If the batter hits a *fly* ball out of the playing area, how many runs are automatically scored?

(a) 2 (b) 4 (c) 6 (d) 8

6. If the batter hits a *ground* ball out of the playing area, how many runs are automatically scored?

(a) 2 (b) 4 (c) 6 (d) 8

7. The sequence of six balls a bowler throws in one direction is called a(n)

(a) innings (b) over (c) strike (d) wide

8. If the bowler throws a ball that is out of reach of the batter this illegal throw is called a

(a) foul (b) ball (c) strike (d) wide

9. The two pieces of molded wood that rest on top of the wickets
are called
(a) bails (b) wickets (c) pins (d) goal posts

True or false. Circle the correct answer.
10. The batter in cricket must carry his bat when running. T   F
11. The bowler can bend his elbow when he throws
    to the batter.   T   F
12. There are balls and strikes in cricket.   T   F
13. There are nine innings in a cricket match.   T   F
14. There are double plays in cricket.   T   F
15. The batter must run when he hits the ball.   T   F
16. If a ball the bowler has thrown gets past the wicket
    keeper, the batters can run.   T   F

Of the following, four are legal ways to get a batter out in cricket.
Circle the four legal ways (#17-20).

   1. The bowler strikes out the batter.
   2. A fielder catches a fly ball hit by the batter.
   3. The bowler throws the ball past the batter and hits his wicket.
   4. A fielder hits the batters wicket when the batter is over the
      popping crease.
   5. The batter hits his own wicket while batting.
   6. The batter fouls off three straight pitches.
   7. A fielder tags a batter when the batter is running.

(Answers:1. d; 2. c; 3. c; 4. a; 5. c; 6. b; 7. b; 8. d; 9. a; 10. T; 11. F;
12. F; 13. F; 14. F; 15. F; 16. T; 17-20: 2, 3, 4, 5.)

1. *Batting Skills Evaluation*
Equipment and set-up: One bat. One tennis ball.

Procedure: Student assumes normal batting position, facing, and
about ten yards away from, a wall.
The teacher (or another student) drops a tennis ball four feet in
front of the batter. The batter tries to hit the ball, which he must do
on the first bounce. Repeat 10 times.

Scoring: One point for each hit.
Maximum possible score: 10 points

2. *Bowling Skills Evaluation* (Diagram #4)
Equipment and set-up: One wicket, without bails, a 4'x4' marker, (a piece of cardboard can be used) and rubber softball.

Place the marker six feet in front of, and directly in line with the wicket.

Procedure: From behind a line twelve yards in front of the wicket, the student bowls five times, underarm, at the wicket, trying to hit it by first bouncing the ball on the marker.

Scoring: Two points for each pitch that hits the marker.
One point for each pitch that hits the wicket.

Maximum possible score: 15 points

3. *Fielding Skills Evaluation (Diagram #5)*
Equipment and set-up: One wicket, without bails. Five tennis balls. Stop-watch.

Place the tennis balls on the floor in a straight line with the wicket, two yards apart from each other.

Procedure: Starting from a line one yard in front of the first ball, the student, on the teachers signal, runs to the first ball, gathers it, throws it at, and tries to hit the wicket.

As soon as he's released the first ball, he goes to the other balls one after another, gathering and throwing each of them at the wicket.

The student has ten seconds to do this.

Scoring: Five points if the student hits the wicket with the first ball. Four points for the second, three points for the third, two for the fourth, one for the ball closest the wicket.

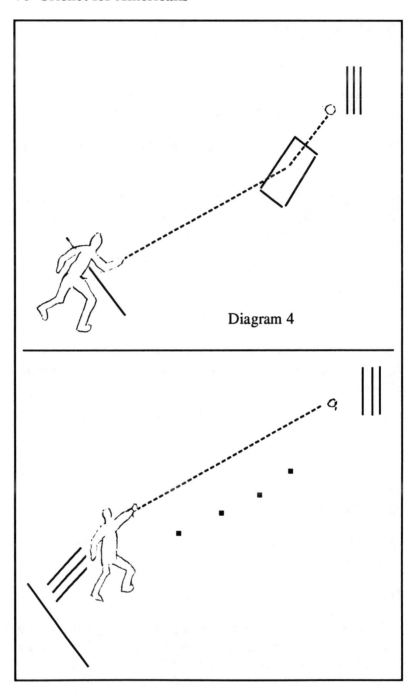

Diagram 4

For each second the student exceeds the 10 second time limit, deduct one point from his score.

Maximum possible score: 15 points

4. Wicket-Keeping Skills Evaluation

Equipment and set-up: One wicket, without bails, bat and tennis ball.

Procedure: Student takes up wicket-keeping position one yard behind the wicket. Another student, with bat, assumes normal batting position at that same wicket.

From a point ten yards away, the teacher (or another student) bowls, underarm, ten times at, but slightly to the side of the wicket, alternating pitches to the off and leg sides.

The batter "shadow bats" to each pitch, i.e., swings at, but purposely misses them. The wicket-keeper tries to catch each pitch, which he must do off the first bounce.

Scoring: One point for each correct catch.

Maximum possible score: 10 points

GRADING: (maximum possible test score: 50 points)

40-50 points	excellent
30-40 points	good
20-30 points	fair
below 20 points	needs improvement

Chapter Eight
Cricket in America

Cricket in the afternoon in my grove with the children.
—Diary entry of Bostonian Amos Lawrence, May 27, 1859

Scratch a baseball diamond anywhere in America and you'll find a cricket ground?

Well, not exactly, but today many scholars of American civilization will tell you early Americans were as likely to have discovered the pleasures of organized bat and ball play on their local cricket grounds as on their neighborhood ball diamonds.

Americans probably never played cricket, even in the game's heyday, just prior to the Civil War, and for a few years at the end of the last century, in any great numbers, but those that did played it, at various times and in various locations, with a devotion and proficiency surprisingly at odds with most contemporary assumptions about American attitudes towards the game.

When, and to what extent, cricket was first played in America isn't known with any certainty, though we do know from William Byrd's diaries that it seems to have been played by Virginia planters on something akin to a "pickup" basis at least as early as the first decades of the eighteenth century (Byrd 144, 146).

The game evidently seemed to have been known to enough American Revolutionary War recruits that George Ewing could record, in his diary, how he and his Continental Army mates passed part of their time at Valley Forge playing "wicket" and, on at least one occassion, even had the honor of playing with General Washington himself (Ewing 47).

With no clearly established team sports traditions of their own, many pre-industrial Americans who were beginning to recognize the value of organized recreation, found, in cricket, an already time-tested and socially acceptable pastime, as enjoyable with the semi-settled residents of such ante-bellum locations as Pittsburg, Kentucky, Cincinnati (which was already supporting, by 1840, at least two cricket clubs, the Western and Queen City) and Chicago (which had a highly partisan inter-city cricket rivalry going with nearby Milwaukee as early as 1851) as it was with the students at Harvard, among them Thomas Wentworth Higginson, whose memories of this game he played in his youth were so dear to the future abolitionist that, half a century later, he pronounced to all those "Who now regard with surprise, or even lift with irreverence, the heavy three-cornered bats and large balls of the game we called cricket...do not know that these comments are like those of Saladin on the heavy sword of King Richard" (Higginson 60).[1]

Cricket enjoyed its greatest following, however, within the burgeoning mid-century urban corridor between New York and Philadelphia, where, according to contemporary press reports, upwards of 5,000 people played the game on a regular basis. (Kirsch 29).

Many of these early cricket players, like those who organized the trendsetting St. George Cricket Club of New York in 1838, were English residents intent on maintaining the ways of the old country, but many others, especially in the Newark and Philadelphia areas, were native Americans looking to establish their own sports identity.[2]

The cricket club that was organized among the students at Philadelphia's Haverford College in 1833, usually accepted as the first exclusively American cricket club, was apparently short-lived, but a virtual explosion of interest in the game among native Philadelphians a couple of decades later ("Everyone plays cricket in Philadelphia," *Porters Spirit of the Times* reported in 1857, "from young men to old") brought forth so many local clubs—the Philadelphia Cricket Club in 1854, the Germantown and Young America clubs a year later—that the city was, even at that time, secure in its status as the "Cricket Capital of America."

These ante-bellum years were clearly flush times for American cricket, but even by this period, America's trail-blazing bat and ball sport was beginning to lose ground to a newcomer on the national sports scene, baseball, and even, by a twist of irony, was about to contribute plenty of "cross over" help to this still young, undeveloped game.

A talented young bowler from the St. George Cricket Club, Harry Wright, who began dabbling in baseball about this time, brought to Cincinnati's local ball club, the Red Stockings, for whom he had accepted the job of player/manager after the Civil War, the "scientific" batting and specialized field placement tactics he knew from cricket, contributing factors to the team's spectacular undefeated national tour of 1869, which left little doubt, by its conclusion, about baseball's vast potential as a professional sport.

Along with the nuts and bolts of playing technique, cricket would also bequeth to early baseball something of its literary spirit (by way of New York cricket scorer and correspondent Henry Chadwick, whose life-long journalistic support for baseball helped mold its image as an American sport), as well as its organizational impetus (by way of Amsterdam, New York, cricketer Nick Young, whose twenty-five year career as president/secretary of the National League all began with the Civil War baseball game he joined in because "it looked like cricket for which his soul thirsted" (Irwin 12+).[3]

Like many others at that time, these baseball pioneers recognized that this relatively simple, quick transition type of ball game was far more approachable to most Americans than England's technically advanced and time consuming sport. A series of catastrophic defeats, in 1859, at the hands of a touring All-England cricket team, which totally outclassed the local opposition in New York, Philadelphia and Rochester, further damaged cricket's efforts to hold its American converts by projecting an image of a game Americans could never play well (*Frank* 305).

By the end of the Civil War, it was clear that cricket was never going to be a broad-based American sport,[4] yet this failure as a sport of mass appeal was able to insure its survival with that segment of American society less tolerant of the abuses that crept into baseball, especially the professional game.

The New Yorkers who got together and formed the Staten Island Cricket and Baseball Club in 1872, "based upon the broadest and most liberal interpretation of the term 'gentleman' and 'amateur'," weren't really interested in playing baseball as much as they were in having in the city a far more responsive cricket organization than the moribund old St. George Club (Clay 102).

The Philadelphia teenagers who organized the Merion Cricket Club in 1865 were even more emphatic about the purity of their club's purpose by successfully turning back an early attempt to convert their organization into a baseball club, the decisive meeting adjourning with a resolution that the baseball equipment purchased in anticipation of this change "be sold off as quickly as possible" (*The Merion* 4).

The members of New Jersey's Seabright Lawn Tennis Club found the sport to be so compatible to their recreation interests, that they persuaded club officials to sod their cricket ground with turf imported all the way from England. The club, which, in 1885, officially became the Seabright Lawn Tennis and Cricket Club, was particularly well known for the interest its women members took in cricket (Prentice).[5]

Cricket did not seem to be as socially prominent a sport in Pittsburg as it was in these eastern cities, but, on the competitive level, its local team was reportedly "as good as any in the country" between 1883 and 1884, and was able to win the patronage, for a few years, of the Carnegie family (Patterson 653).

Following the lead of their Pennsylvania and New Jersey neighbors, a number of prominent Baltimore residents also organized a cricket club for their city in 1876 (Miller 40). The organization, located in the fashionable suburb of Mt. Washington until real estate development forced it to relocate onto the premises of the Baltimore Country Club in 1903, was never, apparently, fertile ground for high quality cricket, though English batting star Gilbert Jessop, during a visit to the city in 1897, found its medium pace bowler K. Mallinckrodt to be one of the most difficult he'd ever played against (Jessop 134).

In the Boston area, where cricket seems to have been long in favor with the New England temperament (the sport was on Emerson's short list of the games recommended for the properly educated young man) (Emerson 6: 140-44; 10: 130-44), the Longwood Cricket Club, which had spun off from the old Boston Cricket Club in 1877, counted a number of ex-baseballers among its members, including future Hall of Famer, George Wright, Harry's brother, who had "left the diamond," and returned to cricket, it was said, "owing to the abuses which crept into the national game" (*Boston* 2).

The Brookline located club, long notorious for its treacherous pitch and short boundaries, was the flagship organization for a surprisingly broad network of late nineteenth-century New England cricket clubs, which extended, at one time or another, to just about every area factory town from Lowell to Pawtucket (Roffe 251-54).

The St. Louis Cricket Club's unprecedented 2500-mile national tour in 1873 couldn't save the game in that city from retreating into permanent obscurity in a corner of Forest Park (where, however, it lives on to this day) (*St. Louis Dispatch*, 7 Aug 1873: 4, *St. Louis Dispatch* 3 Sept. 1873: 4),[6] but the Chicago Cricket Club revived so strongly after its reorganization in 1876 that it was able to undertake a highly successful national tour of its own by 1882 (Andreas 681-2; *Chicago Times* 16 Aug. 1882: 2; *Chicago Times* 10 Sept. 1882: 6).

The Penninsular Cricket Club, for many years Detroit's primary club, also found a new life, after 1890, when it was absorbed and maintained as the cricket section of the prominent Detroit Athletic Club (Patterson 653).

As a college sport, cricket seemed poised, for a brief period after the Civil War, to spread far beyond its traditional strongholds of Haverford College and the University of Pennsylvania.

Representatives from these two schools, which had played America's first intercollegiate cricket match in 1864, got together with delegates from the cricket clubs of Harvard, Columbia, Princeton, and Trinity College to formally establish, in 1881, the Intercollegiate Cricket Association, one of the country's earliest intercollegiate sports organizations (*New York Times* 27 April 1881: 8).

Though plagued through the years with a highly unstable membership (Trinity, Princeton and Columbia dropped out after the first year, Cornell briefly entered a team at the turn of the century, Yale and Johns Hopkins never made good on their intentions to join), this curious sports assocation[7] proved to be surprisingly long-lived, crowning its last champion as recently as 1924.

Many of these collegiate teams drew their players from a number of American secondary schools also closely identified with cricket.

A well-worn cricket path ran, for a few years, from the playing fields of St. Pauls, a boys prep school in Concord, New Hampshire, where cricket had been, from the beginning, "the great game of the school," to the cricket grounds of Harvard, a route traveled by Owen Wister, who's career eventually took him from the management of the Harvard Cricket Club to the authorship of the grandaddy of all Westerns, *The Virginian*. [8]

Germantown Academy was probably Philadelphia's most famous cricket playing school (it once let out classes so its students could watch their classmate William C. Morgan play in a match against a visiting Australian team) and, not surprisingly, the dominant power in the city's turn-of-the-century high school cricket league, though two other local schools, William Penn Charter and Central High, the city's public high school, also frequently turned out strong teams (Lippincott 19; Edmonds 251, 259).

The Wisconsin boys prep school, Racine College, seems to have been an even more dominant local power, once claiming to have gone twenty-five years without losing a match (Lester 94).

At least two private girls schools, Pelham Hall in New York, and Rosemary Hall in Wallingford, Connecticut, also played cricket for a few years at the end of the last century. Spirits evidently ran so high among the girls during their inter-school matches (quite possibly the first school-level girls sports events in American history), the *New York Times* reported the excitement "would have done justice to a Yale-Harvard football match" (*New York Times* 15 Nov. 1896: 8).

No less surprising than America's continued interest in England's national pastime during this period, was the country's popularity as a venue for international play.

More than two dozen first-class cricket teams, from all corners of the cricket world, toured the United States in the half century following the Civil War, often playing their matches in the most unlikely of locations and conditions.

A trio of popular Irish amateur teams brought the spectacle of international cricket to such out-of-the-way locations as Syracuse (1879), Pittsburg (1888) and Lowell, Massachusetts (1892).

Australia's national team twice played in Detroit, their star all-rounder Hugh Trumble falling victim, during the team's second visit in 1893, to what their captain George Giffin claimed was one of the most spectacular catches he'd ever seen on a cricket field (Giffen 91).

Albert Trott's Australian team, in 1896, declined an invitation to play in Minnesota, but did get as far West as Chicago, where they beat a local team that had in its lineup two former White Sox players Cap Anson and Fred Pfeffer (*Chicago Tribune* 8 Oct. 1896: 8).

Robert Fitzgerald's team of English amateurs played the final match of its 1872 on a water logged ground in Boston, while Alfred Shaw's English professionals ended their 1881 tour on San Francisco's rundown, rock strewn "recreation" ground (Fitzgerald 287; Shaw 65-66).

Richard Daft's team of English professionals took some time off from their tour of 1879 to play a few games of baseball, a game they found to be far more challenging than they expected (*Beadles* 46-47). The batters on E.J. Sanders English team were as impressed, during a break in their 1886 tour, with the curve balls of the Philadelphia pitchers, as the Philadelphia baseball batters were with Buckland's slow bowling (Proctor 181, 192-93).

In only one place, however, Philadelphia, did these touring teams ever encounter any serious opposition.

The Quaker City had, over the years, shown sporadic flashes of first class form (it played Australia's test team to a surprisingly even draw in 1878, and even managed to beat Thornton's English team in 1885), but only after its impressive win over Lord Hawke's English amateurs on the Germantown Cricket club's newly opened grounds in 1891, was the city able to maintain this form on anything like a consistent basis.

From that time, and over the next two decades, representative Philadelphia teams, which always played under the name of "The Gentlemen of Philadelphia," were able to win at least a match or two from most foreign teams that visited the city. They beat Australia's test team by an innings on two occassions, in 1893 and

1896, and won, outright, their series with Frank Mitchell's Oxbridge team in 1895, and Bernard Bosanquet's English team in 1901.

None of this would likely have been possible without the close and unusually critical support the game received from many segments of turn-of-the-century Philadelphia society. Crowds of seven or eight thousand spectators, "ranging from millionaires coaching parties and box holders...to newsboys," (Pleasants, *From* 145) routinely filled the stands of the city's "Big Four" cricket clubs, Philadelphia, Germantown, Merion and Belmont, during international matches. Thousands more who could not be there in person, which, according to Haverford College cricketer Henry Pleasants Jr., was "nearly every adult male in the business and professional district of the city," closely followed the progress of the match on the front pages of the *Public Ledger*.

This image as a sport for the serious amateur athlete was also able to win over to cricket converts in other areas of late nineteenth-century America.

Some of the country's better known sporting clubs at that time—the New Jersey and Berkeley Athletic Clubs in the New York area, the Michigan Athletic Club in Detroit and Toledo's Outdoor Club in Ohio—established in-house teams during this period, as did, if probably on a less serious vein, Bloomingdale's, the New York Jockey Club and the Metropolitan Insurance Company (Chadwick 43-4; *New York Times* 21 Aug. 1894: 3; 4 April 1895: 6; *New York Tribune* 5 July 1893: 5; *New York Tribune* 23 June 1895: 5; *New York Tribune* 5 Jan. 1896: 8; *Detroit Free Press* 5 May 1891; *Detroit Free Press* 6 May 1893).

The *American Cricket Annual*, a publication started up by New York cricketer Jerome Flannery in 1890, and continued as a volume in the Spalding Sports Guide series up to the First World War, was clearly indulging in a little wishful thinking by claiming, in its 1896 issue, that cricket was now the country's "leading amateur summer past time" (*American 1896* 5), but we do know that the Spalding Sports Store in Chicago was receiving, by that time, cricket equipment orders from as far away as Duluth, Minnesota, Ironwood, Michigan, and Paris, Texas (*American 1892, 102*).

For reasons that are, to this day, not entirely clear, these many regional pockets of cricket interest never seemed able to successfully work for the cause of their game on anything beyond a local scale.

Representative teams from Boston, New York, Philadelphia, Baltimore, Pittsburg, Detroit and Chicago did attempt to organize among themselves a national cricket "championship" in 1891 (Wharton 172-80), but turf politics, distances and Philadelphia's towering superiority over everyone else (the city beat Chicago in the finals by an innings and 359 runs!) killed the competition after only one year. Later attempts to bring a workable unity to American cricket turned out so poorly that one frustrated official wrote to the *American Cricketer* in 1903 that "it would be easier to write to London...than to get together the members of the American Association" to resolve their differences (*American Cricketer* 15 Jan. 1903: 8).

Philadelphia, for one, was looking much further afield for its competition anyhow. After several years in the planning, the city finally managed to undertake, in 1897, its first strictly first-class English tour, over the course of which its highly erratic and unpredictable team ineffably established the city's reputation as the unknown quantity of Edwardian cricket.

English critics didn't seem to know quite what to make of these weekend American amateurs, who could, one match, fall to a very weak side like Oxford University or Hampshire and then, the very next, turn around and play one of the country's top drawer clubs, like Yorkshire or Nottinghamshire, almost dead even.

The critics were unanimous, however, in their opinion that the Philadelphians had on their team at least one player talented enough to walk into the starting lineup of just about any first-class English club—their opening bowler John Barton King.

The English were particularly intrigued with the way this American could make "the ball swerve in the air after the manner of the baseball pitchers" (*Wisden* 1898: 303) as they described it. In itself, this type of bowling was nothing new—Yorkshire's George Hirst could bowl something like it—but King was the first player who seemed able to do it without any appreciable loss of pace or discernible change in his bowling motion.

He almost singlehandedly won Philadelphia's match against Sussex, taking, on a perfectly true pitch, seven first innings wickets, including that of the world's then number one batter, Prince Ranjitsinhji, for a token thirteen runs, which was three more than he conceded in taking the combined wickets of three other English batting greats that summer, Yorkshire's F.S. Jackson, Somerset's Lionel Palairet, and Surrey's Bobby Abel.

King's heroics notwithstanding, Philadelphia's debut on the English first-class cricket scene was hardly impressive (the side only won two of its fifteen matches, with four drawn) but its second visit, six years later, was, in almost every respect, a completely different story.

King had, by this time, developed into a genuine world-class all-rounder, assigned to open his team's batting as regularly as its bowling, while John Lester, "whose services," the London published *Cricket* magazine claimed ("Chats" 23 July 1903: 289), "not a single English county would not be glad if it could avail itself of," proved to be a more than capable captain in place of the retired George Patterson.

Though still susceptible to the occassional bad outing, the Philadelphians, this time around, rarely found themselves overmatched, as the six county sides they defeated, at times quite impressively, that summer realized.

By tours end even the most sceptical English critics were favorably comparing them to some of the Australian sides they'd seen, others even saw in the way these Americans never gave up on even the most seemingly unreachable boundary hits, a standard to which all English cricketers should aspire (*American Cricketer* 15 Sept. 1903: 160-61).

Back home, these results were interpreted as America's long overdue debut onto the stage of big-time cricket. The *New York Times* saw in them America's rise to "permanent supremacy in the cricket world," with the likelihood of a full-fledged test match between the United States and England just around the corner (16 Aug. 1903: 12).

They were expectations Philadelphia could not live up to during its third, and final, first-class English tour in 1908.

Though this was the only Philadelphia team to have the

satisfaction of beating a team selected by the Marylebone Cricket Club, headquarter club of English cricket, and of seeing King, still "as individual in style," *Wisden* noted, "and as persevering as ever" (*Wisden* 1909: 351), on top of the English first-class bowling standings by seasons end, its sub-five hundred record left little doubt the tenuous progress of American cricket had come to an end.

Even more ominous at the time was the game's declining grass-roots following back in Philadelphia. Most professional class Philadelphians now preferred to fulfill their recreation needs with a couple of hours of tennis, golf or bicycling rather than a long afternoon of cricket, something that was always good up to about four o'clock, but after that, the old international Arthur Wood even admitted, "there is practically no interest at all" ("Chats" 26 Nov. 1903: 450).

Beginning in 1905 the number of matches played in the city went into a precipitous decline, leaving in its wake a rising number of abandoned games, uncompleted schedules and closed down clubs, including Belmont, Kings old club, which sold its grounds and disbanded in 1913.

Worst of all, no-one seemed to know what to do about it. To quicken up the game for American tastes, some clubs experimented, for a while, with the idea of alternating batting and fielding at the fall of every third second innings wicket, à la baseball; others tried the experiment of equally dividing between teams second innings batting time.

Neither seemed able to stem the game's continued decline.

If the right formula for American cricket ever existed, Philadelphia, for all its years of conscientious devotion and attention to the game, just couldn't seem to find it.

A number of older veterans, along with a final generation of talented juniors, kept Philadelphia on the international cricket map for a few more years. King came out of semi-retirement a few months shy of his thirty-ninth birthday and showed he was still one of the world's most dangerous bowlers by leading Philadelphia past Australia's national team in 1912. But the Germantown Cricket Club's upset of another, much stronger, Australian side a year later, was the last time an American team would ever play cricket on a first-class basis, and within barely a decade of this, even Philadelphia, where the old ante-bellum cricketer Robert Waller was certain cricket had "taken so deep a root that it can never be uprooted" (Wister 142), had stopped playing the game altogether.

American cricket did survive its Philadelphia demise.

The game continued to find a following in most large metropolitan areas of the country, as it does to this day, and even continued to attract, periodically, the missionary attention of foreign teams. Australia's test team undertook an extensive tour of the United States and Canada in 1932, as did the Yorkshire County Cricket Club in 1964 and teams selected by the Marylebone Cricket Club in 1967 and 1982.

Through the efforts of expatriate Englishman John Marder, a United States Cricket Association came into existence in 1961, an organization that even managed, a few years later, to revive the old United States-Canada cricket series, which had been, with the exception of several periods of inactivity, annually played between 1844 and 1912.[9]

But the game would not survive as an American institution, only as an ethnic enclave for expatriate foreign cricketers, who, however well-intentioned in their efforts to translate the game to their hosts, have always been strangely ineffective to this end.

It's a state of affairs that, despite all the promises of the past, seems unlikely to change in the forseeable future.

Notes

[1]For ante-bellum cricket in the Midwest, see A.T. Andreas, *History of Chicago,* vol. 2 (New York: Arno, 1975) 613-14: Soeren Brynn, "Some sports in Pittsburgh During the National Period, 1775-1860." *Western Pennsylvania Historical Magazine*, vol. 52 (1969) 71-77.

[2]For cricket's popularity among Americans in Newark, see George Kirsch, "The Rise of Modern Sports: New Jersey Cricketers, Baseball Players and Clubs, 1845-60." *New Jersey History* Spring/Summer 1983: 60.

[3]An in-depth discussion of the relationship between cricket and early baseball can be found in Robert Lewis "Cricket and the Beginnings of Organized Baseball in New York City." *International Journal of the*

History of Sport Dec. 1987: 315-32.

⁴'A very thoughtful, but by no means definitive, analysis of cricket's decline as an American sport during this period can be found in Melvin Adelman's *A Sporting Time: New York City and the Rise of Modern Athletics, 1820-1870* (Urbana: U of Illinois P, 1986).

⁵For women's cricket at Seabright, see *Public Ledger* 30 July 1888: 6.

⁶See also Caroline Loughlin, *Forest Park* (St. Louis: University of Missouri Press, 1986): 217.

⁷For intercollegiate cricket in America, see Henry Chadwick, "Cricket At Harvard." *Outing* Aug. 1890: 415-16; Allen Thomas, "Haverford College Cricket." *Outing* June 1896: 236-40; Frank Presbrey, *Athletics at Princeton: A History* (New York: Presbrey Co., 1901): 20, 23, 30, 557-61; Archibald Graham, *Cricket at the University of Pennsylvania* (Burlington: Privately printed, 1930).

⁸For cricket at St. Pauls see Tom Melville "De Gustibus Non Est Disputandum: Cricket At St. Pauls School and a Note on the Structual/Character Debate in American Cricket." *International Journal of the History of Sport* April 1992: 105-10.

⁹The history of this long running sports event is recounted in John Marder's *The International Series: the Story of the United States vs. Canada at Cricket.* (London: Kaye & Ward, 1968).

Works Cited

American Cricket Annual for 1892. 1893 (NY: Weeks Sport).

American Cricket Annual for 1896. 1897 (NY: Flannery).

American Cricketer. 15 Jan. 1903.

American Cricketer. 15 Sept. 1903.

Andreas, A.T. *History of Chicago.* 3 Vol. New York: Arno P, 1975.

Beadles Dime Base-ball Player. New York: Beadle Co., 1880.

Boston Evening Transcript. 10 July 1892.

Byrd, William. *The Secret Diary of William Byrd of Westover.* Richmond: Dietz P, 1941.

Chadwick, Henry. "Cricket in the Metropolis." *Outing* April 1891: 43-44.

"Chats on the Cricket Field: Dr. J.A. Lester." *Cricket* 23 July 1903: 289-90.

"Chats on the Cricket Field: Mr. A.M. Wood." *Cricket* 26 Nov. 1903: 449-50.

Chicago Tribune. 8 Oct. 1896.

Clay, Charles. "The Staten Island Cricket and Baseball Club." *Outing*

Nov. 1887: 101-112.

Detroit Free Press. 5 May 1891.

Detroit Free Press. 6 May 1893.

Edmonds, Franklin. *History of the Central High School of Philadelphia.* Philadelphia: Lippincott Co., 1902.

Emerson, Ralph Waldo. *Works.* Vol. 6 and vol. 10. Boston: Houghton, Mifflin, 1904.

Ewing, George. *The Military Journal of George Ewing.* New York: Privately Printed, 1928.

Fitzgerald, Robert. *Wickets in the West.* London: Tinsley, 1873.

Frank Leslie's Illustrated Weekly 5 Oct. 1859.

Giffen, George. *With Bat and Ball.* London: Locke Co., 1897.

Higginson, Thomas W. *Cheerful Yesterdays.* NY: Houghton, 1968.

Irwin, Will. "Baseball Before the Professionals Came." *Colliers.* 8 May 1909: 12+.

Jessop, G.L. *A Cricketers Log.* London: Hodder & Stoughton, 1926.

Kirsch, George. "American Cricket: Players and Clubs Before the Civil War." *Journal of Sport History* Spring 1984: 28-49.

Lester, John. *A Century of Philadelphia Cricket.* Philadelphia: U of Pennsylvania P, 1951.

Lippincott, Horace M. *A History of Germantown Academy.* Camden: Lippincott, 1935.

The Merion Cricket Club, 1865-1965. Philadelphia: The Club, 1965.

Miller, Mark. *Mt. Washington: Baltimore Suburb.* Baltimore: GBS Pubs., 1980.

New York Times. 27 April 1881.

New York Times. 21 Aug. 1894.

New York Times. 4 April 1895.

New York Times. 15 Nov. 1896.

New York Times. 16 Aug. 1903.

New York Tribune. 5 July 1893.

New York Tribune. 23 June 1895.

New York Tribune. 5 Jan. 1896.

Patterson, George S. "Cricket in the United States." *Lippincott's Magazine* 50 (1892): 649-660.

Pleasants, Henry. *From Kilts to Pantaloons.* West Chester: Temple, 1945.

―――― "When Philadelphia Played Cricket." *Philadelphia Forum* May 1947: 12-14.

Porters Spirit of the Times 23 May 1857.

Prentice, Bernon. *History of the Seabright Lawn Tennis and Cricket Club.* New Jersey: Privately Printed, 1937.

Proctor, R.A. "Baseball and Cricket," *Longmans Magazine* Vol. 10 (1887), 181-93.

Roffe, Will. "Cricket in New England and the Longwood Cricket Club." *Outing* June 1890: 251-54.

Shaw, Alfred. *Alfred Shaw Cricketer: His Career and Reminiscences* (London: Cassell, 1902) 65-66.

St. Louis Dispatch. 7 Aug. 1873.

St. Louis Dispatch. 3 Sept. 1873.

Wharton, Thomas. "Inter-City and International Cricket in America." *Outing* June 1892, 172-180.

Wisden Cricketers Almanack. London: Wisden Co., 1898.

Wisden Cricketers Almanack. London: Wisden Co., 1909.

Wister, William Rotch. *Some Reminiscences of Cricket in Philadelphia Before 1861.* Philadelphia: Allen, 1904.

Chapter Nine
How Cricket is Organized Around the World

Cricket's transformation from a rural, pre-Victorian, South-of-England recreation, into the recognized team sport of the English speaking world, has made the game somewhat unique.

Other sports, like basketball, may be more popular on a world wide basis, but they're often played under distinct, sometimes conflicting, systems (in basketball's case, the American and international).

The world's other major bat and ball sport, baseball, has found a home from the playgrounds of Korea to the sandlots of Venezuela, but at its highest competitive level, remains a sport dominated by a single country.

Cricket's Anglo-Saxon uniformity of laws, playing traditions and customs, on the other hand, has contributed not only to the development of close international cooperation among, but also competitive parity between, the culturally diverse countries in which cricket is most popular.

The International Cricket Council

The official forum for all this diverse and far-flung cricket activity is the International Cricket Council, a representative organization, headquartered in London, of thirty-five recognized cricket federations, which hold their membership in the ICC under one of four categories:

(1) Foundation membership—reserved for the organization's charter members, England and Australia.
(2) Full membership—reserved for those countries in which first-class (i.e. professional level) cricket is played. Currently there are eight full members; England, Australia, South Africa, the West Indies, India, Pakistan, New Zealand and Sri Lanka.

89

(3) Associate membership—reserved for those countries where cricket, though not played professionally, is recognized as being "firmly established and organized." There are currently nineteen associate members, including the United States.

(4) Affiliate membership—reserved for those countries where cricket is recognized as being played "in accordance with the laws of cricket," but not on a highly organized basis. Currently there are eight affiliate members; Bahamas, France, Italy, Japan, Nepal, Germany, Belgium and Switzerland.

Under its expressed mandate to work "for the development, coordination, regulation and promotion of the game of cricket world wide," the ICC assumes a broad range of responsibilities. It confirms first-class tours among its full members, establishes qualification standards for first-class matches, players and umpires, periodically reviews, in consultation with its members, the laws of the game, and administers an international coaching fund.

The ICC is also responsible for organizing and administering the game's "showpiece" event, the World Cricket Cup, first played in 1975 and held every four years since then.

Since 1979, the competition has been played on a two division plus knock out format among the ICC's full members along with the winner of a qualifying tournament played among the associate members.

Similar in purpose to, but completely unaffiliated with, the ICC is the governing body of women's cricket, the *International Women's Cricket Council,* currently headquartered in Christ Church, New Zealand.

Membership in the IWCC is also held on a "full" or "associate" basis, qualification for the former requiring not less than 100 active women players, the later a modest 25. Since 1973, the IWCC has also had its own world cup.

England
For much of its history, English cricket looked to a single club, London's *Marylebone Cricket Club* (always referred to as simply the "MCC"), for its direction and leadership.

Originally organized In 1787 as a club for well-to-do London amateurs, the MCC gradually evolved, over the next century, into an exclusively administrative organization responsible for overseeing the country's first class cricket, a position it assumed by virtue of its recognized role as the sole arbiter of the laws of the game.

In 1903 the MCC assumed the all-important responsibility for selecting teams to represent England internationally, and, a year later, further extended its influence over the country's domestic cricket with its self-appointment as chair of the *Advisory County Cricket Committee.*

In 1909 the MCC even began to extend its influence internationally, as the sponsoring party to the *Imperial Cricket Conference*, an organization established that year to coordinate cricket contacts between England, Australia and South Africa.

Never free from criticism for its autocratic hold on the game, and increasingly pressured by the organizational and financial complexities of modern, post-World War cricket, the MCC finally began to decentralize its control of world cricket in the 1960s.

The old Imperial Cricket Conference was revamped and became the International Cricket Conference in 1965, the year it first admitted associate members. The Advisory County Cricket Committee also underwent reorganization, emerging, in 1968, as the *Test and County Cricket Board*, a semi-autonomous body responsible for administering all first-class cricket in England. Another administrative body, the *National Cricket Association*, was delegated responsibility for promoting and organizing English cricket on the amateur level.

No longer at the helm of world cricket, the MCC, nonetheless, continues to exert considerable influence over the game. It houses both the Test and County Cricket Board and the National Cricket Association at its headquarters (and home since 1814) Lords Cricket Ground, and, by statute, appoints the chairman of, and underwrites two-thirds of the budget for, the ICC, which also has its offices at Lords.

Above and beyond any of its purely administrative functions, the MCC continues to enjoy unrivaled prestige in world cricket as the recognized guardian of the game's good name and reputation.

Administratively, all first-class cricket in England is, today, under the jurisdiction of the *Test and County Cricket Board* (always referred to as the "TCCB"), a representative body of England's seventeen professional cricket clubs (Durham will become the eighteenth in 1992), along with the MCC and the *Minor Counties Cricket Association* (an organization that represents the country's "semi-pro" clubs).

The TCCB not only organizes, administers and regulates all first-class competition among its members, it is also responsible for organizing all test matches played in England and for selecting teams to represent England in test matches abroad. Its day-to-day responsibilities cover everything from the enforcement of the organization's drug policy to the negotiation of broadcast rights to English cricket.

England's first-class cricket season, which starts in late April and finishes in early September, consists of four separate competitions.

During the week, clubs play their matches for the *County Championship*, a straight twenty-two match round robin, multi-day competition, the winner of which has, historically, always been looked on as England's national cricket "champion."

To satisfy the growing demand for shorter matches, however, these clubs also compete in three weekend limited overs competitions: the *NatWest Trophy*, a sixty over knock out competition, sponsored by the National Westminster Bank; the *Benson & Hedges Cup*, a fifty-five over, four division competition, and the *Sunday League*, a forty-over round robin competition, until recently sponsored by Refuge Assurance.

In organization and structure, England's professional cricket clubs are very different from American professional sports clubs.

All are geographically inalienable, "non profit distributing" associations, directly governed by their members through elected committees, not transferable "franchises" under the control of a few private individuals.

Individual membership fees (the smaller clubs may have as few as 5,000 members, the larger clubs as many as 20,000), are, even in an era of television rights and sponsorship fees, still an important source of income for most English cricket clubs, many of whom can also tap into money raised by their "Supporter

Groups" (i.e., fan clubs) through such non-cricket activities as football pools and lotteries.

The balance of a professional cricket club's revenues will come from its share of test match, national sponsorship and broadcast fees, distributed to each club by the TCCB, as well as from the sale of local advertising and sponsorship rights.

Like other professional sports enterprises, England's first-class cricket clubs are often highly unpredictable financial operations, susceptible to their team's on-field fortunes and the generosity of sponsors. Most clubs fluctuate, year to year, from loss to modest profitability, though the Leicestershire County Cricket Club, which made money an unprecedented ten years in a row during the seventies, has shown that long term profitability is certainly possible.

By tradition, English cricket clubs were expected to staff their teams with predominantly local talent, an arrangement that, despite its paternalistic intentions, for many years severely restricted the career options of most cricketers. Although every amateur English cricketer is, technically, a "free agent" (English cricket has no American style amateur "draft," nor any American style minor league "farm system"—the minor county English cricket clubs are all autonomous organizations), residency requirements, as well as a long-standing policy, now abandoned, that barred a player from moving from one club to another for a better financial arrangement effectively meant most professional cricketers spent their entire careers with their home county.

Following the lead of professional athletes in other sports, professional cricketers have, in recent years, become much more conscious of their market value, hiring agents and showing a greater willingness to move from one team to another for better financial returns. Today it is no longer unusual for a top international cricketer, given all forms of available income—team salary, test match and sponsorship fees, plus bonus fees for winning individual competitions (a much larger share of a professional cricketers income than that of a professional American athlete)—to be able to draw an annual six figure income, certainly nothing comparable to the mega-salaries of American professional athletes, but a vast improvement from the 1960s, when a professional cricketer could expect to earn little more than that of the average skilled worker.

Since its organization in 1968, the *Cricketers Association,* England's professional cricket players union, has also greatly improved the lot of the average first-class cricketer, by winning for its members a minimum wage and pension plan.

England's seventeen first-class cricket clubs vary widely in tradition, strength and quality of facilities.

By virtue of having won the County Championship more often than any other club (29 times), the *Yorkshire County Cricket Club* enjoys a standing and reputation in English cricket roughly comparable to the Yankees or Dodgers in American baseball.

The club, which makes its home at Headingley, a well appointed, if somewhat undistinguished, cricket ground in Leeds, also takes special pride in having produced more international class English cricket players (most notably F.S. Jackson, Herbert Sutcliffe, Sir Len Hutton and, more recently, Geoff Boycott) than any other county, not unexpected for an organization representative of England's largest and, by general consensus, most cricket intent county.

Somewhat ironically, Yorkshire's insistence upon enlisting only local talent for its sides (the club, for example, rarely employs foreign players, as most other English clubs now routinely do), has been a contributing factor to the once proud club's transformation from a gatherer of championships, long feared by opponents for its "warlike and intolerant" play, into a semi-permanent resident of the second division since the late sixties.

The Philadelphians themselves ran head on into this inhospitable "blue collar" Yorkshire spirit during their stop here in 1897, the Americans having to run the gauntlet of both abusive spectators and partisan umpiring to claim for themselves a highly credible draw with the county that summer.

Another of England's more "fashionable" clubs, the *Lancashire County Cricket Club,* plays its home matches at the magnificent Old Trafford cricket ground in Manchester. The ground itself is a fine balance of the traditional and the modern;its stately, old nineteenth-century pavilion, down whose steps players descend, as Neville Cardus once wrote, "like a white waterfall," nicely complimented by recently added skyboxes and state-of-the-art enclosed stands.

Some of cricket history's most memorable moments have taken place here, such as Australia's heart-stopping three run test match win over England in 1902, and Jim Lakers world record nineteen wickets in a single test match, taken off Australia in 1956, a feat as honored in cricket as Don Larson's World Series perfect game in baseball (pitched, coincidentally, that same year).

Philadelphia played here twice, losing to Lancashire in 1897, but beating the county in 1903, a match in which King returned the impressive second innings figures of 9 wickets for 62 runs.

Trent Bridge, another of England's "four star" cricket grounds, just south of Nottingham, is the home ground of the *Nottinghamshire County Cricket Club*. The spacious, six-acre site, whose pavilion exhibits one of the finest collections of cricket memorabilia in existence, is probably best known for its large, imposing scoreboard.

Though "Notts" has, through much of its history, always been one of England's stronger clubs, they always seemed to have their hands full with Philadelphia. The county struggled to hold the Americans to a draw in 1897, lost its first match of the season to them in 1903, and had to overcome a first-innings deficit to beat them in 1908.

The *Warwickshire County Cricket Club* has never enjoyed a reputation as one of England's premier clubs, but its home grounds, Edgbaston, is generally recognized as being one of the finest cricket facilities in the world. Located in a suburb of Birmingham, the ground has some of the most luxurious sports accommodations in England, including a modern, fully equipped indoor practice facility.

In what was widely acclaimed as the best all around showing of their tour, the Philadelphians beat Warwickshire here in 1897, but lost to the county, by seven wickets, on their return visit in 1903.

The *Gloucestershire County Cricket Club*, whose home grounds are just off Nevil Road in Bristol, will always be remembered as the club of cricket's most famous player, William Gilbert Grace (1848-1915), who spent his entire forty-year career with the county.

Grace is frequently referred to as "the Babe Ruth of cricket," a comparison that does not often endear itself to cricket purists, but which, in at least one respect, is totally appropriate.

Like Ruth, who elevated baseball into a crowd-pleasing batting extravaganza with his dazzling long ball hitting, Grace transformed cricket into a magnetic, high-scoring spectacle with his prolific, forceful, forward play.

"I don't like defensive strokes," he was always fond of saying, "you can only get three off 'em!"

Though most of his cricket records (over 50,000 career runs, and nearly 3,000 career wickets) have since been broken, he remains, to this day, the most enduring and recognizable symbol of the greatness of cricket as an English institution.

With Grace in harness, Gloucester beat Philadelphia here in 1897, but its innings and 26 run loss to the same opponents in 1903 remains on the record books as the worst ever suffered by a county side at the hands of an American team.

The *Somerset County Cricket Club*, whose large, but rather unpretentious home grounds lie in the shadow of St. James church in Taunton, has enjoyed, over the years, the services of some of England's finest batters, such as Lionel Palairet, who played for them before the First World War, and, more recently, the heavy-hitting Ian Botham. For all this, the county remains one of only three clubs that's never won the County Championship.

The *Worcestershire County Cricket Club*, on the other hand, has recently been enjoying one of the most prosperous periods in its history, the back-to-back County Championships it won in 1988 and 1989 having contributed a dose of on-field excitement to the otherwise aesthetic calm of the club's home grounds in Worcester, which, nestled along the banks of the Severn, shadowed by the distant Malvern Hills, and overlooked by the city's majestic cathedral, has long been regarded as one of the loveliest in all of England.

An injury-ridden Philadelphia side lost to Worcester here in 1903, but the Americans exacted revenge five years later when Arthur Wood's 132 second innings runs carried them past the county by 95 runs.

Two first-class cricket clubs play in the London area.

North of the Thames, the *Middlesex County Cricket Club* makes its home at the famous Lords Cricket Ground in St. Johns Wood.

Though by no means the largest, or even best equipped cricket ground in England, Lords stands as the richest in prestige and tradition, as revered a symbol of the spirit of English cricket as Yankee Stadium is of American baseball. Just about every famous cricketer has, at one time or another, passed through its stately turn-of-the-century pavilion, whose Long Room, with its extensive collection of cricket art and memorabilia, doubles, for all intents and purposes, as cricket's "Hall of Fame." Its annual mid-summer test match, described by one writer as the "high noon in the cricketing year," rounds out, along with Ascot and Wimbledon, the triumvirate of big-time English sports events.

For many years no more than an also-ran in county cricket, Middlesex itself has, under the captaincy of sometime English test captain Mike Gatting, developed into one of England's more consistently successful clubs, rarely going through a season, over the past decade, without winning at least one competition.

London's other first-class club, the *Surrey County Cricket Club*, geographically no farther from Lords than a jaunt across the Thames, may as well be worlds away in character and personality. Whereas a heavy, officious air of aristocrative reserve often hangs over Lords, Surrey's noisy, urban ground, the Kennington Oval, always seems to exude an atmosphere "not partially," as Neville Cardus found it, "but wholly democratic and homespun." Surrey supporters are also quick to remind visitors that it was on their ground, and not Lords, that the very first test match was played on English soil (against Australia in 1880).

Surrey can make other claims on English cricket history, having won the County Championship more often—seventeen times—than any other club except Yorkshire, including a record seven straight titles between 1952 and 1958. All this, however, hasn't been much consolation for their supporters who have seen Surrey, over the last few decades, eclipsed as a force in English cricket.

Surrey hosted Philadelphia on three occasions, beating the Americans, with some difficulty, in 1897 and 1908, but losing an exciting match to them in 1903, when King bowled their draw intent final batter with only minutes left on the clock.

In the South of England, the *Kent County Cricket Club* plays at the tranquil St. Lawrence Cricket Ground just outside Canterbury, the club's home since 1847, famous for the 150-year-old lime tree standing within its boundaries.

After losing to the Philadelphians in 1903, Kent made a return visit to America that Fall, and completed a successful four match tour, the first, and, to this day, only time a county side has ever played first-class cricket in the United States.

Two other "Channel Clubs," the *Hampshire County Cricket Club*, which plays its home matches on a very pretty ground in Southampton, and the *Sussex County Cricket Club*, whose home ground at Hove is situated only a few hundred yards from the sea, have, in recent years, been overshadowed by their nearby neighbor at Chelmsford, the *Essex County Cricket Club*, which has emerged, since its initial county championship in 1979, as one of England's strongest county sides.

Other clubs have not left as strong an imprint on English cricket.

The *Leicestershire County Cricket Club* has brought only one county championship to its supporters at Grace Road in Leicester, that in 1975, while the *Derbyshire County Cricket Club*, domiciled off Nottingham Road in Derby, lives with the dubious distinction of being the only county side to have ever gone through an entire season without a win or a draw (0-17 in 1920). Twelve years earlier the county was even easy pickings for Philadelphia, when King, "varying his pace with great skill and repeatedly deceiving the batsmen in the flight of the ball," as *Wisden* described it, "had the Derbyshire team at his mercy."

The *Northhamptonshire County Cricket Club*, whose home grounds are in a heavily industrialized area of Northampton, has come close a couple of times, but, like Somerset and Sussex, has yet to win a county championship. Wales only first-class cricket organization, the *Glamorgan County Cricket Club*, which plays most of its home matches at Sophia Gardens in Cardiff, did not lose a single match during its championship year of 1969, but since that time has seldom been able to avoid second division finishes.

Australia

First-class cricket in Australia is organized by the *Australian Cricket Board*, a representative council, located in Melbourne, of the country's six state cricket associations, New South Wales, Victoria, Queensland, South Australia, Western Australia and Tasmania.

In addition to its first-class administrative duties (selecting and contracting players for the national team, negotiating broadcast and advertising rights to Australian cricket, among other things), the ACB also plays a prominent role organizing and promoting cricket on the amateur level through a national coaching program and several junior competitions. It even markets, under a separate subsidiary, a popular plastic "wiffle" ball cricket set.

Though never as respected an organization in world cricket as the MCC and, historically, somewhat slow to fall in step with such emerging trends as limited overs cricket, the ACB has, nonetheless, shown itself to be, with its aggressive pursuit of cricket sponsors and liberal use of modern marketing methods, the most successful in adopting to the game's increased commercialization.

Australia's first-class cricket season, which runs from November to the end of March, is, like England's, a collage of several distinct competitions.

The oldest (first played in 1892), and still considered the most important, is the *Sheffield Shield*, a double round-robin, plus one match final, multi-day competition among the country's six professional teams.

These same clubs also participate in a short limited-overs competition, in past years sponsored by McDonalds, currently by *FAI Insurance,*

The most popular event of the Australian cricket season, however, is the *World Series Cricket Cup*, an annual twelve match, plus best of three final, limited-overs triangular competition between Australia and two visiting national cricket teams.

Though now very much an accepted part of the Australian cricket scene, World Series Cricket represented, on its inception in 1977, a radical departure for not only Australian, but all of world cricket.

As a private initiative of Australian media mogul Kerry Packer, the competition not only presented, at that time, a direct challenge to established world cricket authority (in the beginning, both the ICC and the ACB waged a bitter and expensive legal battle against the WSC program), its introduction of such American sports "gimmicks" as colored uniforms, night matches, and white cricket balls, though now widely accepted, was looked on as a direct challenge to the game's traditional image.

There are six first-class cricket teams in Australia, all representative sides of their respective state cricket associations.

Of these clubs, *New South Wales* probably has the strongest claim to the title, "Australia's team," having won the Sheffield Shield far more often than any other club, including a record nine straight times between 1953 and 1961.

New South Wales also enjoys the prestige of playing its home matches at the Sydney Cricket Ground, often considered the finest all around cricket facility in the world, though the ground is probably best known not for any distinct architectural or playing feature, but its "Hill," formerly an open, grassy section of the stands, now seated over, notorious (like Cleveland Stadium's "dawg pound," to which one visiting American sportswriter compared it) as the gathering place of the most raucous and vocal spectators.

Above and beyond this, New South Wales is also remembered as the club of, arguably, the greatest cricket batter of all time, Sir Donald Bradman (1908-), the second name from cricket history every American should be familiar with.

If cricket batsmanship first emerged as a multi-dimensional art with W.G. Grace, with Don Bradman, it matured into its highest state of technical perfection.

Other batters, at other times and locations, had been able to amass large scores, but Bradman was the first who seemed able to do it, against any kind of bowling, and under just about any condition, with such mechanical consistency and physically exhausting precision that he was often, it was said, too tired to unstrap his own batting pads by games end.

Once asked the secret of his success by an English sports writer, he replied, "I never visualize the possibility of *anyone* getting me out."

Critics have now and then faulted him for reducing the art of batsmanship to a joyless automation, but no-one has ever questioned the greatness of its results: career first-class and test batting averages of, respectively, 95.14 and 99.94 runs, records that most cricket experts believe will never be broken.

Victoria, another of Australia's more "storied" clubs, enjoys the benefit of playing its home matches at the world's largest cricket ground, the Melbourne Cricket Ground (always referred to as the "MCG"), located in Jolimont, a suburb of Melbourne.

With its large, state-of-the-art visual scoreboard, and multi-tiered seating, the spacious facility, site of the 1956 Olympics, is one of only a handful of cricket grounds in the world capable of projecting an American-type stadium atmosphere.

One of the largest crowds to ever watch a cricket match (some 90,000) packed the grounds in 1961 for a match between Australia and the West Indies. Here also Victoria, in a match against New South Wales in 1926, set the all time record for most runs in an innings, 1,107. Lest any American over-hastily think they see proof, in that total, of a serious offensive imbalance in cricket, it should immediately be pointed out that this same Victorian team, in their return match with New South Wales four weeks later, was skittled out for a grand total of only 35 runs!

Up in Brisbane, *Queensland* plays its home matches at the Wooloongabba, or "The Gabba" as its commonly called. The stark, rather unattractive ground, site of cricket's first tied test match between Australia and the West Indies in 1961, underwent extensive improvements in the 1970s, but its exposure to frequent sub-tropical showers and popularity with Australia's most informal crowds, still leaves the visitor with the impression, as it did Neville Cardus, that "this is cricket in Bret Harte's Roaring Camp."

To most Australians, however, Queensland is known as the only club, along with the much younger Tasmania, never to have won the Sheffield Shield, even though the "Maroons" have enjoyed, through the years, the services of some of Australia's most talented batters, including current Australian test captain Alan Border.

Western Australia, on the other hand, has enjoyed considerable competitive prosperity in recent years. Long known as a limited-overs power, the club has also recently begun to pick up a fair share of Sheffield Shield titles, including three straight from 1986 to 1988.

The club plays its home matches at the "WACA," an acronym for the Western Australia Cricket Association, a small, privately owned facility in the center of Perth. The ground is best known for its lively, bouncey pitch (long the happy hunting ground of the club's former world-class fast bowler, Dennis Lillee, and more recently Terry Alderman) and its "Freemantle Doctor," a refreshing, heat breaking breeze that regularly blows in from the sea late each afternoon.

South Australia plays at the Adelaide Oval, generally considered to be the most "English" of Australia's first-class cricket grounds because of its cozy atmosphere and proximity to the city's picturesque cathedral. Its old-world atmosphere, however, has been somewhat compromised with the recent addition of a new $10 million grandstand.

Another small, picturesque ground, the Bellerive Oval in Hobart, is the home ground of *Tasmania*, a club that has yet to make any real mark on Australian cricket since its elevation to full first-class standing in 1982.

West Indies

First-class cricket in the West Indies is under the administration of the *West Indies Cricket Board of Control*, whose official functions are "to plan, promote and organize cricket and also to arrange overseas tours with other international cricketing bodies." There are twelve representatives on the board, two from each of the six territories whose cricket associations field first-class teams; Barbados, Guyana, Jamaica, Trinidad & Tobago, plus the Leeward and Windward Islands.

The West Indies cricket season, which begins in January and ends in April, consists of two first-class competitions, the *Red Stripe League*, a four day round-robin competition, and the *Geddes Grant One-Day Tournament*, the island's annual limited-overs competition.

Of the six cricket-playing territories, *Barbados* has shown itself to be in a virtual class by itself. The island, generally considered to be the most cricket-sophisticated in the Caribbean, has not only won more domestic cricket championships than any other territory, it has probably produced more first-class cricket players on a per capita basis than any other geographic area of the world.

From this island has also come the third figure in world cricket every American should know, Sir Garfield, "Gary" Sobers (1936-), generally recognized as the game's greatest all-rounder, and locally celebrated, in the lyrics of one calypso singer, as "the greatest cricketer on Earth and Mars."

If a comparable figure must be identified from American sports, it would probably be Sober's close contemporary from baseball, Willie Mays, at least to the extent both represented, in their respective sports, the hereto unseen phenomenon of the athlete who could, literally, "do it all."

To the record books, Sobers is known as the holder of test cricket's all time single innings scoring record, 365 runs, made against Pakistan at Jamaica's Sabina Park in 1958. Many, however, will tell you they best remember him as the captain of the Rest of the World team who gathered himself before the harsh criticism of a first innings duck against Australia in 1971 and played, in his second innings, one of the most explosive double centuries in cricket history.

Barbados plays its home matches at Bridgetown's Kensington Oval, like most Caribbean cricket grounds, a small, basically "no frills" facility. The ground gained international attention during the sixties for the antics of "King Dial," an outrageously costumed local "super fan" who would incite the crowd with his mock-imperial entrance at the beginning of each test match.

Jamaica has never played as influential a role in, nor has it contributed as many first-class players to, West Indian cricket as one would expect from the Caribbean's largest and most populous cricket playing island, though it has always taken special pride in having given the West Indies its first genuine world class cricketer, George Headley.

With its recent expansion, Jamaica's home ground in Kingston, Sabina Park, is no longer the tiny, congested playing area it used to be, but still compact enough to intimidate visiting teams when the din of the crowd, as one local sportswriter described it, "comes in layers, like storm-blown breakers crashing against the Northeast coast."

On this ground as well a team of pioneering American cricketers, gathered from the more prominent clubs of Philadelphia, Boston and New York, finished up, in 1888, history's first international tour to the West Indies with a loss to an All-Kingston team.

These same Americans also made a stop at the Caribbean's largest and best equipped cricket ground, Queens Park, then, as now, the home ground, of *Trinidad and Tobago*. Situated at the foot of some lushly vegetated sub-tropical hills in Port of Spain, the attractively landscaped area is also generally recognized as the most picturesque in the West Indies.

Guyana plays its home matches at the Bourda ground in Georgetown, a ground known for its exceptionally fine pitch, though it didn't prevent the American cricketers of 1887-88 from knocking out the All-West Indian team they played here for only 19 first innings runs!

The *Leeward Islands*, which have recently begun to host international matches at the Recreation Ground in St. John's, Antigua (a facility well maintained by inmates from an adjoining prison), are probably best known to the cricket world for their native son, Viv Richards, the most talented cricket batter of his generation.

The *Windward Islands* distribute their home matches between Queens Park in St. George, Grenada, Mindoo Phillip Park in Castries, St. Lucia, and Arnos Vale in St. Vincent.

South Africa
After a twenty-year exile, South Africa was officially welcomed back to the international cricket community with its reinstatement, late in 1991, as a full member of the ICC, a decision that turned on the constitutional commitment of that country's recently organized *United Cricket Board of South Africa* to promote cricket in South Africa "without distinction based on color, race, creed, religion or sex."

Under its new constitution, the UCB of SA is also responsible for organizing, controlling and coordinating all first-class cricket played among the eleven South African provincial cricket bodies which field first-class teams.

The first-class cricket season in South Africa, which begins on October 1 and runs through March 31, consists of four competitions.

Representative teams from the country's six major provinces, Western Province, Eastern Province, Natal, Orange Free State, Northern Transvaal and Transvaal, play for the *Castle Cup* (formerly known as the Currie Cup), the country's oldest and most important multi-day competition. The country's second tier provincial teams, Griqualand West, Boland, Western and Eastern Transvaal, have their own competition, the *Presidents Cup*.

There are also two limited overs competitions, the *Nissan Shield* and the *Benson and Hedges Tournament,* though neither's organized on a strictly first-class basis.

South Africa maintains four test match grounds.

The oldest, St. George's Park in Port Elizabeth, is the home ground for Eastern Province, a club that, despite the services, from 1960 to 1978, of South Africa's arguably greatest cricketer, Graeme Pollock, has never won the Castle/Currie Cup.

Kingsmead, in Durban, home ground of Natal Province, is probably best known as the site of the famous "timeless" test match played here between South Africa and England in 1938/39, when the two teams tried the experiment of playing a test match without any time limit. Ten days and 1,981 runs later, the still uncompleted match had to finally be stopped so the English team could catch their boat home.

Notoriety of a different kind came to Newlands, an attractive, oak tree encircled ground lying at the foot of Capetown's Table Mountain, in 1978, the year its home club, Western Province, broke South African cricket's race barrier by signing on the talented colored player, Omar Henry.

South Africa's other test match venue, Wanderers Stadium in Johannesburg, is the home ground of Transvaal, winner of more Castle/Currie Cup titles than any other South African club. The spacious, imposing facility you see today in Kent Park was built in 1956 as a replacement for the "old" Wanderers ground, which was torn down in 1946 to make way for railroad construction.

Sri Lanka

First-class cricket in Sri Lanka, the youngest of the test playing countries (it became the ICC's eighth full member in 1981), is under the jurisdiction of the Colombo-based *Board of Control for Cricket In Sir Lanka.* The board represents some seventy cricket clubs and organizations, which hold membership on either a controlling or affiliate basis.

The first-class cricket season in Sri Lanka, which runs from August to April, currently comprises three multi-day competitions. The three-day *Lakspray* and five-day *P. Saravanamuttu* competitions are reserved for Sri Lanka's twenty some Division 1 cricket clubs. The third competition, the *Presidents Cup*, is not contested by individual clubs, but by representative sides of the country's six provincial cricket groups, Colombo City, Colombo Suburbs, Southern, Western, Central and Northwestern Provinces.

Over the years, Sri Lanka has organized, with the support of such various sponsors as Honda and GTE, a number of limited overs competitions, but they have almost all been junior level affairs.

Most of Sir Lanka's test matches are played in Colombo, on the city's three first-class grounds; Maitland Place, home of the *Sinhalese Sports Club*, one of the country's oldest and perennially strongest cricket clubs, Maitland Crescent, a completely separate ground, home of another strong Sri Lankan club, the *Colombo Cricket Club*, and the P. Saravanamuttu Stadium. The last mentioned ground will always hold a special place in the history of Sri Lankan cricket as the site of the country's first victory in a test match, over India, by six wickets, in 1985.

India

The administrative body of Indian cricket is the *Board of Control for Cricket In India*, an organization that represents the country's numerous local cricket associations, usually grouped, for competitive purposes, into five geographic zones, East, West, North, South and Central.

India, whose cricket season runs from October to April, supports two major first-class competitions.

The oldest and most prestigious, if somewhat unwieldy,

competition, the *Ranji Cup*, named after Prince K.S. Ranjitsinhji, the country's first great cricketer, is organized on a two-tier format. Clubs start out by playing a single round robin with the other first-class teams in their zone (there's four first-class clubs in the East, five in each of the other zones), with the top two finishers from each zone then advancing to a final knock-out round.

The other major competition, the *Duleep Trophy*, inaugurated in 1961, and named after another famous early Indian cricketer, K.S. Duleepsinhji, is played as a straight knock-out tournament among representative teams from each of the five zones. The limited overs *Wills Tournament*, started in 1977, does not yet qualify as a strictly first-class competition.

There are three major test match grounds in India.

Eden Gardens, in Calcutta, though not the best equipped, is India's oldest and largest test ground. Seats at the huge, concrete stadium are in such great demand for important test matches that those that are made available to the general public usually have to be distributed by lottery. The ground recently set a world cricket attendance record when some 95,000 spectators turned out late in 1991 to watch a limited overs match between India and South Africa.

At the other end of the subcontinent, situated just off Marine Drive in a fashionable area of Bombay, is India's most impressive cricket ground, Brabourne Stadium. The facility, named after Bombay's last British governor, Lord Brabourne, who donated reclaimed land for the stadium in 1936, is actually an all-purpose sports complex that, in addition to its fine cricket area, incorporates a swimming pool, squash courts and even a hotel for visiting teams.

Brabourne is also the home ground of the *Bombay Cricket Club*, one of India's strongest clubs (it once won the Ranji Trophy fifteen years in a row!), and the one for which India's greatest modern cricketer, and world record holder for most career test runs (10,122), Sunil Gavaskar, played until his recent retirement in 1987.

India's other major cricket ground, Wankahede Stadium, is also its most modern, though the facility has never been able to completely shake the controversy that surrounded the decision to build it, in 1975, barely a mile from Brabourne.

In addition to these locations, test matches have also been played at Delhi, Kanpur, Bangalore and Madras. Chidambaram Stadium in the last mentioned city gained overnight fame in 1986 when the test match played there between India and Australia ended in a tie, only the second in cricket history.

Pakistan

First-class cricket in Pakistan is administered by the *Board of Control for Cricket In Pakistan*, a representative body of the numerous District Cricket Associations active within each of the country's four provinces. The board's honorary president, secretary and treasurer are all government appointees, an arrangement that has, not surprisingly, frequently subjected the country's cricket to considerable political intrigue.

Pakistan, whose cricket season runs from October to March, supports three first-class competitions. The four-day *Patrons Trophy* is contested on a divisional plus knock out basis among some thirty teams affiliated with Pakistan's largest private companies, cities and government institutions. The teams that advance to the knock out round of this competition automatically qualify for the *Quaid-e-Azam Trophy* (i.e., "Great Leader," a reference to Mohammed Ali Jinnah, architect of Pakistani independence), also a four-day competition, played on a straight round robin basis, as well as for the *Wills Trophy* the country's limited overs competition.

Test matches are played in Faisalabad, Islamabad, Sialkot, Multan and Peshawar, but Lahore's Gaddafi Stadium, a huge concrete structure, named in honor of Libya's well-known leader, and Karachi's National Cricket Stadium are the preferred match locations.

President Eisenhower was a guest at the later ground, a virtual oasis on the fringe of the Sind Desert a few miles outside of Karachi, for a match between Pakistan and Australia in 1959, to date, the only time an American president has ever attended a test match.

New Zealand

First class cricket in New Zealand is organized and administered by the *New Zealand Cricket Council*, a twelve-member representative committee of the country's six major cricket associations, Auckland, Wellington, Canterbury, Otago and Northern and Central Districts.

From the end of November to mid-February, representative teams from these associations compete in the country's two first-class competitions, the three-day *Shell Trophy* which is played on a double round robin format, and the *Shell Cup* a limited overs competition played on a league plus knock-out basis.

New Zealand has four stand-out cricket grounds.

On the South Island, in Dunedin, there's Carisbrook, home ground of Otago, and, in Christchurch, Lancaster Park, the time honored ground of Canterbury, the club of New Zealand's most famous cricketer, Sir Richard Hadlee, who, at the time of his retirement in 1990, held the world record for most career test wickets (415).

On the North island, built over an old lake bed, is Basin Reserve, Wellington's home ground, and, in Auckland, Eden Park, the country's largest cricket ground and the one on which New Zealand got its first test match win, over the West Indies, in 1956.

It was also the ground on which, a year earlier, the "Kiwis" managed to make, in their match against England, only 26 first innings runs, still the world record low score for a single test innings.

Plate 1. "Just a game where I throw the ball and you try 'n hit it." But one so dynamically unconstricted that it allows, as shown here, the "pitcher" to take a run-up and the batter to even hit the ball backwards.

Plate 2. Out! Bowled! Not three often judgemental strikes, but just a single no-doubt-about-it pitch onto the wicket, like here, is all it takes to get a cricket batter out.

Plate 3. Out! Caught! The frequency of purely defensive swings makes shallow catches, like the one being taken by the diving fielder at the right, as regular an occurrence in cricket as deep fly catches in baseball.

Plate 4. Out! Stumped! The batter, who's missed the ball while over the popping crease, tries to get back by touching down his bat, but its too late, as the wicket-keeper's already taken the ball and hit his wicket.

Plate 5. Out! Run out! Even by lunging his bat out ahead of him, the near batter couldn't get over the popping crease in time to beat out a direct hit on his wicket by the fielder charging in from the right.

Plate 6. The sight every cricket batter dreads; the umpire's raised index finger—which has just told this unlucky batter he's been given out LBW.

Plate 7. Nowhere is the wonderful diversity of cricket batting probably more evident than in the "sweep" shot, where the batter, shown here, actually drops to one knee to hit the ball around to his left.

Plate 8. A common cricket sight when a fast bowler's operating; the wicket-keeper playing back, anchoring a cordon of slip fielders poised and ready to snatch up the "foul ticks" expected from this type of bowling.

Plate 9. The highly conspicuous palm tree tells you this is cricket somewhere in the Caribbean, specifically, at Kensington Oval, Barbados' largest cricket ground.

Plate 11. Wanderer's Stadium in Johannesburg, South Africa's largest cricket ground, at the time of its opening in 1956.

Plate 12. A Scene from the match between all-New York and Australia, on the grounds of the St. George Cricket Club in Hoboken in 1882. Ten years earlier Robert Fitzgerald and his English amateurs had found the site—not to be confused with the club's famous ground at Elysian Fields—

GRAND CRICKET MATCH!
MILWAUKEE vs. CHICAGO.

☞   THE RETURN MATCH between the Milwaukee
and Chicago Cricket Clubs will come off on the ground
above Spring st. Hill, on Monday next, Oct. 3d. Play to commence at 10 o, clock A.M.

Ample Refreshments will be provided on the ground—
The two clubs will dine together in the evening, at the
Cricketer's Retreat, opposite the U.S. Hotel. Tickets to the
Dinner $1.00—to be had of the Steward's.

All lovers of manly sport are invited to come and see
the game.   J. BARNETT, Stewards of the
                             W. BIGNALL,   Mtl. Club
October 1, 1853.   d2t

Plate 13. "The day was lovely, an Indian summer haze so sufficiently clouded and
warmed the atmosphere that it gave that dreamy beauty to the landscape so pecu-
liar to the West," was how the Milwaukee newspapers described the idyllic setting for one late summer match between Milwaukee and Chicago during the early
1850s, notices for which, like the above, bear testimony to the event's status at the
time.

te 14. Surrey's spacious home ground, Kennington Oval. The Laker Stand is just to the left of the pavilion, the cen-
building supporting the two white sightscreens.

Plate 15. A birds-eye view of a sold out Melbourne Cricket Ground, largest sports stadium in the Southern Hemisphere.

Plate 16. The calm before the storm. Even at pre-game, the steely concentration that made him the world's greatest cricket batter is already etched upon Don Bradman's face.

Plate 17. Gaddafi Stadium, Pakistan's largest cricket ground, during, it appears, a slow day.

Glossary

all-rounder

A player who's good enough to hold a starting place on a team as both a batter and bowler.

around the wicket

Bowling on the same side of the wicket as one's dexterity. i.e., a right hander bowling on the right side of the wicket is bowling "around the wicket."

Ashes

Trophy symbolic of Anglo/ Australian cricket supremacy. So called because Australian supporters, in ceremonially burning some bails after their test team had beaten England in 1882, claimed to have reduced English cricket "to ashes." Since then, a test series between the two countries is always played "for the ashes."

"attacking field"

Fielding configuration designed to get batters out by inducing them to try and hit balls past fielders playing very shallow. Usually seen at the beginning of matches when a fast bowler is operating.

back up

The non strikers "lead off." i.e., as soon as the bowler has released

127

the ball, the non striker, anticipating a run, will normally go over his popping crease and take a few steps towards the opposite wicket.

bails
Two small, cylindrical pieces of molded wood, 4 3/8 inches long, that rest in grooves on top of the wicket. At least one must be knocked off to get a batter out bowler, stumped, run out or hit wicket.

"barracking"
Australian expression for vocal, raucous, spectator behavior intended to intimidate the opposing team.

batting crease
Another name for the popping crease (q.v.).

beamer
Slang for a fast, head-high, full toss.

block hole
The spot on the ground where the striker, when ready to hit, normally rests the heel of his bat.

bodyline
Tactic in which the bowler, under the pretext of bowling at the leg stump, bowls at the batter. The term has come to be associated with the England/Australia test series of 1933/34, when England captain Douglas Jardine instructed his bowlers to bowl this way.

bouncer	A delivery thrown at the batter, but pitched short and fast, so it will bounce up at the batters head. Cricket's "brush back" pitch.
boundary	A four (q.v.) or a six (q.v.) .
bowled	Form of out where the bowler gets a delivery past the batter, hits his wicket, and knocks off at least one bail. Cricket equivalent of a "strikeout."
bowled around the legs	When a batter is bowled by a ball that passes behind, rather than in front of, him.
bowler	The cricket "pitcher."
bowling crease	A line marked parallel to and four feet behind the popping crease (q.v.) that joins the return creases (q.v.). Rule changes in the sixties that required the bowler to have part of his front foot behind the popping crease rather than his back foot behind the bowling crease effectively rendered this marking obsolete.
"build an innings, to"	Said of a batter who makes a high score over a long period of careful, steady play.
bumper	Another name for a bouncer (q.v.).
bye	A run scored from a delivery that was not hit by the bat and did not

hit the batters body. Normally runs are scored this way from deliveries that get past the wicket-keeper. Cricket's "passed ball."

"captains innings"

An outstanding batting performance played by the team's captain from a disadvantageous position. Has become a popular expression for any gritty, determined effort under difficult circumstances.

caught

Form of out where a fielder catches, on the fly, a ball hit by the batter.

caught behind

Short for "caught behind the wicket." The batter's said to be out this way when he "ticks" the ball and it's caught by the wicket-keeper.

century

A batter who scores a hundred runs in a single time at bat has "made a century." A mark of distinction in cricket roughly comparable to rushing for 100 yards in American football.

change over

The fielding team's shift, at the end of each over, to positions correlated to the reversed bowling direction.

"chuck"

Slang term for bowling with an illegal, bent arm motion.

cover

Mid-depth, off side fielding position situated "8:30" from the striker.

cross bat

Batting with a horizontal, baseball-like swing. Used to hit high deliveries.

crumbling pitch

A pitch whose surface is beginning to slightly breakup. Usually considered a good pitch for a spin bowler.

cutter

A type of medium pace delivery whose spin makes the ball bounce into or away from the batter.

dead pitch

A pitch on which the ball bounces low and very straight. Considered a good pitch to bat on.

declaration

A tactical option whereby the batting team can stop batting before all its batters have got up or been put out. Usually done to allow enough time to get the opposing team out.

delivery

Formal term for a cricket pitch.

"double, the"

A player who scores 1,000 runs and takes a 100 wickets in a single season has "done the double."

draw

The official result of any match that cannot, for any reason, be fully completed, regardless of the score. Matches are usually drawn because of interference by the weather, or the expiration of time. Not the same as a tie (q.v.) .

dropped catch

A fly ball that a fielder gets his hands on, but can't hold.

"duck"

Slang term for a batter who gets out without scoring a single run.

extra cover

Mid-depth off-side fielding position situated "8:00" from the striker.

extras

Collective term for all byes, no balls, leg byes and wides.

fall of wicket

An out, always used in reference to the batting side. i.e., "the fourth wicket fell..." means the batting team has made its fourth out.

fast bowler

A bowler who tries to get batters out with sheer, all-out ball speed.

fine

Fielding or batting in more direct line with the pitch. i.e., if a fielder is asked to position himself "finer," he will move more parallel to the pitch. A batter who wants to hit the ball "finer" tries to hit it more parallel to the pitch.

fine leg

Mid-depth, on-side fielding postion situated "1:00" from the striker.

first class   The highest level of cricket. Equivalent to professional level in American sports.

flight   Variation in the height of delivery. i.e., his off-breaks were "well flighted."

follow on   Tactical option available in a two innings match, that allows the team that bats first, if ahead after one full innings by a prescribed number of runs, to reverse the second innings batting sequence.

four   A ground ball hit out of the playing area. So called because it scores an automatic four runs.

full toss   A delivery that reaches the batter on the fly.

googly   An off-break thrown with a motion disguised as a leg-break.

graft, to   To score runs in an unenterprising, "take-whats-given" style.

"grubber"   Slang term for a delivery that's rolled along the ground.

guard, take   A batter's self-positioning in relation to his wicket before starting to bat. He will usually take guard "middle and leg," i.e., line himself up between the middle and leg stumps, or "leg," i.e., in line with the leg stump.

Similar to a baseball batter's positioning himself in relation to the plate.

gully

A shallow, off side fielding position situated "10:00" from the striker.

handled the ball

Form of out where the batter intentionally touches a ball that's in play.

hat trick

When a bowler takes three wickets on three *successive* deliveries.

hit wicket

Form of out where a batter, while batting, hits his wicket, with either his bat or body, and knocks off at least one bail.

"hole out"

Usually said of a batter who's caught from a lazy, looping, fly ball.

hook

Cross bat stroke, used to hit short pitched leg side deliveries, that rise more than shoulder high, in the direction of square leg.

"howzat"

Truncation of "how's that?" the prescribed form of address for all appeals.

innings

A team's turn at bat, but also used to describe an individuals time at bat. i.e., "he played a good innings." Always used in the plural.

innings, win by a   Said of a team that, in a two innings match, has scored more runs in one time at bat, than its opponents have in two.

LBW   Abbreviation for "leg before wicket" (q.v.).

leg before wicket   Form of out where the batter blocks, with his body, a delivery the umpire judges would have hit the wicket.

leg break   A slow delivery whose counter-clockwise rotation makes the ball bounce away from a (right handed) batter.

leg bye   A run scored from a delivery that hits the batters body, but not his bat.

leg side   Another name for the on-side (q.v.).

leg stump   That pole of the wicket closest to the batter.

limited-overs cricket   A type of cricket in which each team is limited, in its time at bat, to a predetermined number of overs.

line and length   Desirable ball placement, where the bowler tries to pitch his deliveries directly at, but far enough from, the wicket to make them difficult for a batter to hit.

	i.e., "he kept a good line and length.
long hop	A delivery pitched so short that it usually reaches the batter more than waist high. Considered an easy ball to hit.
long off	Deep, off-side fielding position situated "7:00" from the striker.
long on	Deep on-side fielding position situated "5:00" from the striker.
maiden	An over in which no runs are scored off the bat.
man of the match	Cricket equivalent of American sports' "most valuable player."
medium pace bowler	A bowler who tries to get batters out with accuracy and ball movement rather than sheer speed.
mid off	Mid depth off side fielding position situated "7:00" from the striker.
mid on	Mid depth on side fielding position situated "5:00" from the striker.
mid wicket	Mid depth on side fielding position situated "4:00" from the striker.
middle stump	The center pole of the wicket.

night watchman

A lower order batter who opens a team's batting when there's only a short time remaining before play ends for the day. A team usually puts a weaker, lower order batter up in this situation to avoid the risk of losing a better, top order batter in the few remaining minutes of play.

no ball

An illegal delivery, most commonly called when the bowler either bends his arm while bowling, steps outside the return creases, or completely over the popping crease. Every no ball results in a penalty run for the batting team and must be taken over.

non striker

The batter not being bowled to.

not out batsman

The batter "left over" after all the other members of his team have been put out. The batting team's innings are over at this point because this last batter, who has no more partners, cannot bat alone.

off break

A slow delivery whose clockwise rotation makes the ball bounce into the (right handed) batter.

off drive

Straight bat stroke used to hit over-pitched deliveries on or just outside the off stump between cover and mid off.

off side
The name assigned to that half of the playing area towards which the striker is facing.

off stump
That pole of the wicket farthest from the striker.

on drive
Straight bat stroke used to hit over-pitched deliveries on or just outside the leg stump between mid-wicket and mid on.

on side
The name assigned to that half of the field behind the striker.

opener
Either of the team's first two batters.

over
A set of six fair deliveries bowled, alternately, from each wicket.

over-pitched
A delivery that's bounced close to the batter. Usually considered an easy ball to hit.

over the wicket
Bowling on that side of the wicket opposite one's dexterity. i.e., a right hander bowling on the left side of the wicket is bowling "over the wicket."

overnight not outs
The two batters up at the end of a days play, who will resume their batting the next time play begins.

pace bowler
Another name for a fast bowler (q.v.).

"pair, make a" Said of a batter who's out for a duck both times in a two innings match.

pitch (1) The official name of the area of the field between the wickets and about as wide as the return creases. (2) the spot on which a bowled ball bounces.

played on Said of a delivery that hits the batter or his wicket after first hitting his bat.

point A mid depth, off side fielding position situated "9:00" from the striker.

popping crease A twelve-foot line marked four feet in front of and parallel to the wicket. The batter must have some part of his bat or body touching behind this line to be safe, or to score a run. Bowlers cannot go over this line until they have released the ball.

pull Cross bat stroke used to hit short-pitched leg side deliveries, that rise lower than shoulder height, towards square leg.

quick single A run beat out from a shallow hit. Something like a cricket "bunt."

rabbit Slang term for a weak, usually bottom-of-the-order batter.

recognized batsman

A player who's on the team for his batting ability.

return creases

Two eight-foot long lines, 8' 8" apart, that run back at right angles from the popping crease towards the wicket. For a delivery to be fair, the bowler's back foot must not go outside these creases.

Roses match

Name for the match between the Lancashire County Cricket Club (red rose) and the Yorkshire County Cricket Club (white rose).

run out

A form of out in which the batter, while going for a run, fails to touch part of his bat or body over the popping crease before the fielding team hits his wicket with the ball and knocks off at least one bail. The cricket equivalent of being caught "off base."

runner

A substitute who runs for a batter unable to run for himself.

shooter

A fast delivery that stays very low after pitching.

short-pitched

A delivery that bounces well in front of the batter.

short run

An incomplete run resulting from a batter's failure to ground part of his body or bat behind the popping crease when running. Any runs "scored" this way are disallowed.

sight screen
An upright, rectangular structure, color contrasted to the cricket ball, located just beyond the boundary, in line with the pitch. Used, just like the dark colored, unused center field seats in a baseball stadium, to help batters pick up the bowled ball from its background.

silly point
Shallow, off side fielding position situated "8:00" from the striker.

six
A ball hit over the boundary on the fly. So-called because it scores six automatic runs. Cricket's "home run."

"sledging"
Australian expression for a fielding team's vocal intimidation of the opposing batters.

slip
Shallow, off side fielding positions situated anywhere between "10:00" and "11:00" from the striker.

"slog"
Slang term for aggressive, but indiscriminate and reckless batting.

slow bowler
Another name for a spin bowler (q.v.).

snick
Another name for a thin edge (q.v.).

spectacles
Another name for "a pair" (q.v.).

spin bowler

A bowler who tries to get batters out with slow, spinning deliveries that take erratic, hard-to-hit bounces.

square

Fielding or batting more at right angles to the line of the pitch. i.e., a batter who's trying to hit the ball "squarer" is trying to hit it straight sideways.

square cut

Cross bat stroke used to hit short-pitched off side deliveries in the direction of point.

square leg

A mid-depth, on side fielding position, situated "3:00" from the striker.

square leg umpire

The umpire at the strikers wicket. So called because he positions himself near the square leg fielder.

sticky wicket

A pitch that's damp but drying out. A difficult pitch to bat on because the ball tends to take very erratic bounces.

stone walling

To bat with the sole intention of not getting out, rather than scoring runs.

straight bat

Hitting with a vertical "golf like" swing. Used to hit low deliveries.

strike rate

A statistical category that measures the average number of runs a batter makes per 100 deliveries. It's calculated by dividing the number of runs a batter scores by the number of balls faced. i.e., if the batter's scored 100 runs on 200 deliveries, his strike rate is 50.

striker

The batter who is being bowled to.

"strong all around the wicket"

Cricket expression comparable to baseball's "able to hit to all fields with power."

stump

The name for each of the wicket's three individual poles. Hence, the wicket is often referred to as "the stumps."

stumped

Form of out where the wicket-keeper hits the batter's wicket with a ball the batter has gone over the popping crease trying to hit, but missed. Something like a "pick off" in cricket.

sweep

Cross bat stroke used to hit slow, leg side deliveries in the direction of square leg.

swing bowler

A bowler who tries to get batters out by "curving" the ball into or away from them.

take a wicket

An out, always used in reference to the bowler, i.e. the expression "bowler X took three wickets" means he got out three batters.

take the shine off the ball　To bat long enough to wear down the opening bowlers, who always start the game with a shiny new ball.

test　International level. i.e., test matches are games between national all-star cricket teams. A test player is a member of such a team.

thick edge　A solid "tick" that sends the ball fairly square.

thin edge　A very slight "tick" that sends the ball very fine.

third man　Deep, off side fielding position situated "11:00" from the striker.

through the gate　Said of a delivery that bowls a batter by passing through the gap between his bat and body.

throws his wicket away　Said of a batter who gets himself out in a foolish, reckless manner.

tie　The official result when both teams have the same number of runs at the completion of their *full* innings. *Not* the same as a draw (q.v.).

"tip and run"　Slang expression for up-tempo, but somewhat free-wheeling cricket. Usually applied to limited overs matches.

trapped

Common expression for being out LBW (q.v.).

turning pitch

A pitch on which the ball tends to "bite" into. Hence, one that's good for spin bowling.

twelfth man

A team's designated substitute.

wicket

The set of three wooden poles, 28" above the ground, together, 9" wide, that function something like "bases" in cricket.

wicket, win (lose) by

How a match won by the team that bats second is always scored, based on the number of batters still to be put out. i.e., a team that had three batters yet to be put out at the time it beat the other teams score has "won by three wicket." If it had four batters yet to be put out, it "won by four wickets" etc.

wicket-keeper

The cricket "catcher."

wide

A delivery that, in the umpire's judgement, cannot be reached by the batter standing in his normal position. Every delivery judged a wide results in one penalty run for the batting team and must be taken over.

yorker

A delivery that pitches behind the popping crease.

Bibliography of Cricket Resources

Books and Magazines

Of the many reference books available on cricket, *Wisden Cricketers Almanack* is by far the most important and respected. Published annually since 1864, this "Bible of cricket" not only provides an exhaustive statistical summary of the years cricket, it also includes, with each edition, insightful articles on the personalities, developments and recent history of the game, many written by leading authorities and area specialists.

The pick of the available cricket periodicals is the *Cricketer International,* published in Tunbridge Wells, England. Though editorially somewhat conservative, and heavily slanted in its coverage towards English cricket, the magazine has been, since its first appearance in 1921, the best single source for keeping in touch with the game around the world.

The most respected history of the game is Harry Altham's two-volume *A History of Cricket* (London: Allen & Unwin, 1962), but readers looking for something with a more international perspective may also want to go to Rowland Bowen's *Cricket: A History of Its Growth and Development Throughout the World* (London: Eyre and Spottiswoode, 1970). A chatty, and more concise treatment of the subject can be found in Trevor Bailey's *A History of Cricket* (London: Allen & Unwin, 1979).

Among the many available general coaching manuals, the *MCC Coaching Book,* first published by Naldrett Press in 1952 and now into its fourth edition, is the "old reliable," though Keith Andrew's *The Skills of Cricket* (Ramsbury: Crowood, 1984) is also very good.

Those looking for more specialized guides can turn to *Alan Knott on Wicket-Keeping* (London: Stanley Paul, 1977) or Geoff Boycott's *On Batting* (London: Stanley Paul, 1980). This later book has a unique composite of action photos printed on the

147

margin of its pages, which, when flipped, actually produce a miniature movie of the author demonstrating the different batting strokes.

Former English test captain Mike Brearley can guide you through the tactical intricacies of the game with his *The Art of Captaincy* (London: Hodder & Stoughton, 1985), while Tom Smith's *Cricket Umpiring and Scoring* (London: Dent, 1980) is a virtual course in itself for anyone interested in this important aspect of the game.

Mention English cricket and you have to talk about the most celebrated writer on the subject, Sir Neville Cardus (1889-1975). The players, events and spirit of English cricket have never been more lucidly and beautifully described than in the prose of this late cricket and music critic of the *Manchester Guardian*. All of his more than half dozen cricket books are worth reading, but many think his *Australian Summer* (Toronto: Nelson, 1937) is the best.

An entertaining account of the day-to-day life of an English professional cricket player can be found in Peter Roebuck's *It Never Rains: A Cricketers Lot* (London: Allen & Unwin, 1984). An inside look of a more serious nature is Geoffrey Moorhouse's *Lords* (London: Hodder & Stoughton, 1983) which delves into the behind the scenes working of England's most famous cricket institution.

For information on cricket Down Under, readers can turn to Jack Pollard's encyclopedic *Australian Cricket: The Game and the Players* (Sydney: Hodder & Stoughton, 1982). Though hard to come by, Herbert Hordern's chatty and humorous *Googlies* (Sydney: Angus & Robertson, 1932), is also worth while reading for Americans if only because of its pen portraits of Philadelphia cricket, which the author, one of the earliest, and, some still say, finest exponents of the googly, became intimately associated with when he took time off from his dental studies at the University of Pennsylvania and joined the Americans on their English tour of 1908.

For New Zealand cricket there's Donald Neely's mammoth *Men In White: The History of New Zealand International Cricket* (Auckland: Moa Pubs., 1985).

Of the surprisingly large number of books available on Indian and South African cricket, readers may want to start with Mihir Bose's highly readable *A Maidan View: The Magic of Indian Cricket* (London: Allen & Unwin, 1986) and *A Century of South Africa in Test and International Cricket, 1889-1989* (Johannesburg: J. Ball, 1989).

The late C.L.R. James' semi-autobiographical *Beyond a Boundary* (New York: Pantheon, 1984) is, in the opinion of many critics, more than just a rich and searching portrait of the meaning of cricket in West Indian society. It's also one of the finest books ever written on a sports related subject.

Cricket's influence upon the early development of America's sporting traditions has recently attracted considerable scholarly attention, most notably in Melvin Adelman's *A Sporting Time: New York City and the Rise of Modern Athletics, 1820-1870* (Urbana: University of Illinois, 1986), and George Kirsch's *The Creation of American Team Sports: Baseball and Cricket, 1838-1872* (Urbana; University of Illinois, 1989).

John Lester's *A Century of Philadelphia Cricket* (Philadelphia: University of Pennsylvania, 1951), presently the only full-length work available on American cricket, should be read in conjunction with Henry Sayen's *A Yankee Looks at Cricket* (London: Putnam, 1956), a loving reminiscence of the golden age of Philadelphia cricket, written by a member of the 1908 team that toured England, and the only American to ever play for the Gentlemen of England, that country's "all star" cricket team.

Audiovisual Aids

Those looking for a good coaching video will find everything they need with *The Game of Cricket*, a five part, state-of-the-art instructional program, available in both film and videotape, that was produced by England's National Cricket Association, with the support of the National Westminster Bank, in 1983.

Two delightful Australian films, *Cricket, Australian Style,* produced in 1974, and the older, but still enjoyable black and white film, *Bat, Ball and Boy,* are non-technical surveys of the game in Australia. The last I heard, both could still be borrowed, without charge, from most Australian consulates.

Equipment

If you happen to be in a cricket-playing country, you'll usually have no further to look than the neighborhood sports store for cricket equipment. If not, you can order directly from the following sports stores that specialize in mail order cricket equipment:

Bourne Sports
Church St.
Stoke-on-Trent ST4 1DJ
Great Britain

Morrant Sports
The Factory
1 Walpole Rd.
South Woodford
London E182 LN

Kingsgrove Sports
247-249 Kingsgrove Rd.
Kingsgrove, NSW 2208
Australia

Museums

Last, but not least, any American who happens to be in the Philadelphia area should not pass up an opportunity to visit the *C.C. Morris Cricket Library*, the "Cooperstown of American Cricket."

Housed in a specially built wing of the Haverford College Library, the collection has on display many photos, portraits and other memorabilia from the golden age of Philadelphia cricket, much of it donated by descendents of former Philadelphia cricketers. The library is currently open to the public on Mondays, Wednesdays and Fridays from one to four p.m., and by appointment with the main library.

THE

LAWS OF CRICKET

(1980 Code)

SECOND EDITION - 1992

_____

OFFICIAL

_____

Copyright MCC 1979

World Copyright Reserved

Reprinted with permission

151

PREFACE

The game of Cricket has been governed by a series of Codes of Law for nearly two hundred and fifty years. These Codes were introduced as indicated below, and were subject to additions and alterations decided by the governing authorities of the time. Since its formation in 1787 the Marylebone Cricket Club (MCC) has been recognised as the sole authority for drawing up the Code and all subsequent amendments.

There can be little doubt that Cricket was recognised as early as 1700, but the earliest known Code was drawn by certain Noblemen and Gentlemen who used the Artillery Ground in London. These Laws were revised in 1755 by 'Several Cricket Clubs, particularly the Star and Garter in Pall Mall'. The next arrangement was produced by 'a committee of Noblemen and Gentlemen of Kent, Hampshire, Surrey, Sussex, Middlesex and London', at the Star and Garter on 25 February 1774. This in turn was revised by a similar body in February 1786.

The first MCC Code was adopted on 30 May 1788 and remained unchanged until 19 May 1835, when a new Code of Laws was approved by the Committee. The 1835 Code, amended from time to time, stood until 21 April 1884, when, after consultation with Cricket Clubs world-wide, important alterations were incorporated in a new version approved at a Special General Meeting of MCC.

By 1939 the 1884 Code of Laws, having been supplemented by the inclusion of many definitions and interpretations in the form of notes, were in need of revision. At the conclusion of the 1939-1945 World War the opinions of controlling bodies and Clubs throughout the world were sought resulting in a new Code being approved at a Special General Meeting of MCC on 7 May 1947. The main changes in the 1947 Code were aimed at clarification and better arrangement of the Laws and their interpretations. This did not, however, exclude certain definite alterations which were designed to provide greater latitude in the conduct of the game as required by the widely differing conditions in which cricket was played.

During the following thirty years a number of changes were required including the publication of five editions of the 1947 Code. During the International Cricket Conference of 1972, MCC suggested the time had come for the Code to be revised and re-written. The aim was to remove certain anomalies, consolidate various Amendments and Notes and to achieve greater clarity and simplification. MCC undertook the task starting in 1974 with the 1980 Code of the Laws being approved at a Special General Meeting of MCC on 21 November 1979. This second edition of the 1980 Code incorporates all the amendments which have been approved during the last twelve years.

Many queries on the Laws, which apply equally to women's cricket as to men's, are sent to MCC for decision every year. MCC as the accepted makers of the Laws, which can only be changed by the vote of two-thirds of the members present and voting at a Special General Meeting of the Club, has always been prepared to answer the queries and to give interpretations on certain conditions which will be readily understood, ie:—

(a) In the case of League or Competition Cricket, the enquiry must come from the Committee responsible for organising the league or competition. In other cases, enquiries should be initiated by a representative officer of a Club, or of an Umpires' Association on behalf of his or her Committee, or by a master or mistress in charge of school cricket.

(b) The incident on which a ruling is required must not be merely invented for disputation, but must have actually occurred in play.

(c) The enquiry must not be connected in any way with a bet or wager.

Since their inception over two centuries ago the Laws of Cricket have stood the test remarkably well. On 1 October 1991 the International Cricket Council (formerly Conference), administered by MCC, implemented an agreed International Code of Conduct. This Code emphasises the responsibility of Captains under the Laws of Cricket to ensure their players conduct themselves within the spirit as well as within the Laws of the Game. The unique character and enjoyment of Cricket depends on all players, at whatever level, continuing to preserve this spirit.

J R STEPHENSON
Secretary MCC

Lord's Cricket Ground
London NW8 8QN
1 January 1992

CONTENTS

LAW 1   THE PLAYERS

1. Number of Players and Captain

A match is played between two sides each of eleven Players, one of whom shall be Captain. In the event of the Captain not being available at any time a Deputy shall act for him.

2. Nomination of Players

Before the toss for innings, the Captain shall nominate his Players who may not thereafter be changed without the consent of the opposing Captain.

NOTES

(a) More or Less than Eleven Players Players a Side

A match may be played by agreement between sides of more or less than eleven players but not more than eleven players may field.

LAW 2   SUBSTITUTES AND RUNNERS:
BATSMAN OR FIELDSMAN LEAVING THE FIELD:
BATSMAN RETIRING
BATSMAN COMMENCING INNINGS

1. Substitutes

In normal circumstances, a Substitute shall be allowed to field only for a player who satisfies the Umpires that he has become injured or become ill during the match. However, in very exceptional circumstances, the Umpires may use their discretion to allow a Substitute for a player who has to leave the field for other wholly acceptable reasons, subject to consent being given by the opposing Captain. If a player wishes to change his shirt, boots, etc., he may leave the field to do so (no changing on the field) but no Substitute will be allowed.

2. Objection to Substitutes

The opposing Captain shall have no right of objection to any player acting as Substitute on the field, nor as to where he shall field; however, no Substitute shall act as Wicket-Keeper.

3. Substitute Not to Bat or Bowl

A Substitute shall not be allowed to bat or bowl.

4. A Player for whom a Substitute has acted

A player may bat, bowl or field even though a Substitute has acted for him.

5. Runner

A Runner shall be allowed for a Batsman who during the match is incapacitated by illness or injury. The player acting as Runner shall be a member of the batting side and shall, if possible, have already batted in that innings.

6. Runner's Equipment

The player acting as Runner for an injured Batsman shall wear the same external protective equipment as the injured Batsman.

7. Transgression of the Laws by an Injured Batsman or Runner

An injured Batsman may be out should his Runner break any one of Laws 33: (Handled the Ball), 37: (Obstructing the Field) or 38. (Run Out). As Striker he remains himself subject to the Laws. Furthermore, should he be out of his ground for any purpose and the wicket at the Wicket-Keeper's end be put down he shall be out under Law 38: (Run Out) or Law 39: (Stumped) irrespective of the position of the other Batsman or the Runner and no runs shall be scored.

When not the Striker, the injured Batsman is out of the game and shall stand where he does not interfere with the play. Should he bring himself into the game in any way then he shall suffer the penalties that any transgression of the Laws demands.

8. Fieldsman Leaving the Field

No Fieldsman shall leave the field or return during a session of play without the consent of the Umpire at the Bowler's end. The Umpire's consent is also necessary if a Substitute is required for a Fieldsman, when his side returns to the field after an interval. If a member of the fielding side leaves the field or fails to return after an interval and is absent from the field for longer than 15 minutes, he shall not be permitted to bowl after his return until he has been on the field for at least that length of playing time for which he was absent. This restriction shall not apply at the start of a new day's play.

9. Batsman Leaving the Field or Retiring

A Batsman may leave the field or retire at any time owing to illness, injury or other unavoidable cause, having previously notified the Umpire at the Bowler's end. He may resume his innings at the fall of a wicket, which for the purposes of this Law shall include the retirement of another Batsman.

If he leaves the field or retires for any other reason he may only resume his innings with the consent of the opposing Captain. When a Batsman has left the field or retired and is unable to return owing to illness, injury or other unavoidable cause, his innings is to be recorded as "retired, not out'. Otherwise it is to be recorded as "retired out".

10. Commencement of a Batsman's Innings

A Batsman shall be considered to have commenced his innings once he has stepped on to the field of play
NOTES

(a) Substitutes and Runners

For the purpose of these Laws allowable illnesses or injuries are those which occur at any time after the nomination by the Captains of their teams.

LAW 3 THE UMPIRES

1. Appointment

Before the toss for innings two Umpires shall be appointed, one for each end, to control the game with absolute impartiality as required by the Laws.

2. Change of Umpire

No Umpire shall be changed during a match without the consent of both Captains.

3. Special Conditions

Before the toss for innings, the Umpires shall agree with both Captains on any special conditions affecting the conduct of the match.

4. The Wickets

The Umpires shall satisfy themselves before the start of the match that the wickets are properly pitched.

5. Clock or Watch

The Umpires shall agree between themselves and inform both Captains before the start of the match on the watch or clock to be followed during the match.

6. Conduct and Implements

Before and during a match the Umpires shall ensure that the conduct of the game and the implements used are strictly in accordance with the Laws.

7. Fair and Unfair Play

The Umpires shall be the sole judges of fair and unfair play.

8. Fitness of Ground, Weather and Light

(a) The Umpires shall be the sole judges of the fitness of the ground, weather and light for play.

(i) However, before deciding to suspend play or not to start play or not to resume play after an interval or stoppage, the Umpires shall establish whether both Captains (the Batsmen at the wicket may deputise for their Captain) wish to commence or to continue in the prevailing conditions; if so, their wishes shall be met.

(ii) In addition, if during play, the Umpires decide that the light is unfit, only the batting side shall have the option of continuing play. After agreeing to continue to play in unfit light conditions, the Captain of the batting side (or a Batsman at the wicket) may appeal against the light to the Umpires, who shall uphold the appeal only if, in their opinion, the light has deteriorated since the agreement to continue was made.

(b) After any suspension of play, the Umpires, unaccompanied by any of the Players, or Officials shall, on their own initiative, carry out an inspection immediately the conditions improve and shall continue to inspect at intervals. Immediately the Umpires decide that play is possible they shall call upon the Players to resume the game.

9. Exceptional Circumstances

In exceptional circumstances, other than those of weather, ground or light, the Umpires may decide to suspend or abandon play. Before making such a decision the Umpires shall establish, if the circumstances allow, whether both Captains (the Batsmen at the wicket may deputise for their Captain) wish to continue in the prevailing conditions: if so their wishes shall be met.

10. Position of Umpires

The Umpires shall stand where they can best see any act upon which their decision may be required.

Subject to this over-riding consideration the Umpire at the Bowler's end shall stand where he does not interfere with either the Bowler's run up or the Striker's view.

The Umpire at the Striker's end may elect to stand on the off instead of the leg side of the pitch, provided he informs the Captain of the fielding side and the Striker of his intention to do so.

11. Umpires Changing Ends

The Umpires shall change ends after each side has had one innings.

12. Disputes

All disputes shall be determined by the Umpires and if they disagree the actual state of things shall continue.

13. Signals

The following code of signals shall be used by Umpires who will wait until a signal has been answered by a Scorer before allowing the game to proceed.

Boundary	-by waving the arm from side to side.
Boundary 6	-by raising both arms above the head.
Bye	-by raising an open hand above the head.
Dead Ball	-by crossing and re-crossing the wrists below the waist.

Leg Bye	-by touching a raised knee with the hand.
No Ball	-by extending one arm horizontally.
Out	-by raising the index finger above the head. If not out the Umpire shall call "not out".
Short Run	-by bending the arm upwards and by touching the nearer shoulder with the tips of the fingers.
Wide	-by extending both arms horizontally.

14. Correctness of Scores

The Umpires shall be responsible for satisfying themselves on the correctness of the scores throughout and at the conclusion of the match. See law 21.6 (Correctness of Result).

NOTES

(a) Attendance of Umpires

The Umpires should be present on the ground and report to the Ground Executive or the equivalent at least 30 minutes before the start of a day's play

(b) Consultation Between Umpires and Scorers

Consultation between Umpires and Scorers over doubtful points is essential.

(c) Fitness of Ground

The Umpires shall consider the ground as unfit for play when it is so wet or slippery as to deprive the Bowlers of a reasonable foothold, the Fieldsmen, other than the deep-fielders, of the power of free movement, or the Batsmen the ability to play their strokes or to run between the wickets. Play should not be suspended merely because the grass and the ball are wet and slippery.

(d) Fitness of Weather and Light

The Umpires should only suspend play when they consider that the conditions are so bad that it is unreasonable or dangerous to continue.

LAW 4   THE SCORERS

1. Recording Runs

All runs scored shall be recorded by Scorers appointed for the purpose. Where there are two Scorers they shall frequently check to ensure that the score sheets agree.

2. Acknowledging Signals

The Scorers shall accept and immediately acknowledge all instructions and signals given to them by the Umpires.

LAW 5   THE BALL

1. Weight and Size

The ball, when new, shall weight not less than 5 1/2 ounces/155.9g., nor more than 5 1/4 ounces/163g: and shall measure not less than 8 13/16 inches/22.4 cm., nor more than 9 inches/22.9 cm. in circumference.

2. Approval of Balls

All balls used in matches shall be approved by the Umpires and Captains before the start of the match.

3. New Ball

Subject to agreement to the contrary, having been made before the toss, either Captain may demand a new ball at the start of each innings.

4. New Ball in Match of 3 or more Days Duration

In a match of 3 or more days duration, the Captain of the fielding side may demand a new ball after the prescribed number of overs has been bowled with the old one. The Governing Body for cricket in the country concerned shall decide the number of overs applicable in that country which shall be not less then 74 six-ball overs (55 eight-ball overs).

5. Ball Lost or Becoming Unfit for Play

In the event of a ball during play being lost or, in the opinion of the Umpires, becoming unfit for play, the Umpires shall allow it to be replaced by one that in their opinion has had a similar amount of wear. If a ball is to be replaced, the Umpire shall inform the Batsmen.

NOTES

(a) Specifications

The specifications, as described in 1 above shall apply to

top-grade balls only. The following degrees of tolerance
will be acceptable for other grades of ball.
(i) Mens Grades 2-4
Weight: 5 5/16 ounces/150g. to 5 13/16 ounces/165 g.
Size: 8 11/16 inches/22.0 cm. to 9 1/16 inches/23.0 cm
(ii) Women's
Weight: 4 15/16 ounces/140 g. to 5 5/16 ounces/150g.
Size: 8 1/4 inches/21.0 cm to 8 7/8 inches/22.5cm.
(iii) Junior
Weight: 4 5/16 ounces/133g. to 5 1/16 ounces/143g
Size: 8 1/16 inches/20.5 cm. to 8 11/16 inches/22.0cm.

LAW 6 THE BAT

1. Width and Length
The bat overall shall not be more than 38 inches / 96.5 cm. in length; the blade of the bat shall be made of wood and shall not exceed 4 1/4 inches / 10.8 cm. at the widest part.
NOTES

(a) *The blade of the bat may be covered with material for*
protection, strengthening or repair. Such material shall not
exceed 1/16 inch /1.56 mm. in thickness.

LAW 7 THE PITCH

1. Area of Pitch
The pitch is the area between the bowling creases—see Law 9: (The Bowling, Popping and Return Creases). It shall measure 5ft./1.52m in width on either side of a line joining the center of the middle stumps of the wickets—see Law 8: (The Wickets).

2. Selection and Preparation
Before the toss for innings, the Executive of the Ground shall be responsible for the selection and preparation of the pitch; thereafter the Umpires shall control its use and maintenance.

3. Changing the Pitch
The pitch shall not be changed during a match unless it

becomes unfit for play, and then only with the consent of both Captains.

4. Non-Turf Pitches

In the event of a non-turf pitch being used, the following shall apply:

> (a) LENGTH: That of the playing surface to a minimum of 58ft. (17.68 m.)

> (b) WIDTH   That of the playing surface to a minimum of 6ft. (1.83 m.)

See Law 10: (Rolling, Sweeping, Mowing, Watering the Pitch and Re-marking of Creases) Note (a).

LAW 8 THE WICKETS

1. Width and Pitch

Two sets of wickets, each 9 inches/22.86 cm. wide, and consisting of three wooden stumps with two wooden bails upon the top, shall be pitched opposite and parallel to each other at a distance of 22 yards/20.12m. between the centres of the two middle stumps.

2. Size of Stumps

The stumps shall be equal and sufficient size to prevent the ball from passing between them. Their tops shall be 28 inches / 71.1cm. above the ground, and shall be dome-shaped except for the bail grooves.

3. Size of Bails

The bails shall be each 4 3/8 inches / 11.1 cm. in length and when in position on the top of the stumps shall not project more than 1/2 inch / 1.3 cm. above them.

NOTES

> (a) Dispensing with Bails
> *In a high wind the Umpires may decide to dispense with the use of bails.*
> (b) Junior Cricket

For Junior Cricket, as defined by the local Governing Body, the following measurements for the Wickets shall apply:

Width	*-8 inches / 20.32 cm*
Pitched	*-21 yards / 19.20 m.*
Height	*-27 inches/ 68.58 cm.*
Bails	*-each 3 7/8 inches/9.84 cm. in length and should not project more than 1/2 inch / 1.3 cm. above them.*

LAW 9 THE BOWLING, POPPING AND RETURN CREASES

1. The Bowling Crease

The bowling crease shall be marked in line with the stumps at each end and shall be 8ft. 8 inches/ 2.64 m. in length, with the stumps in the centre.

2. The Popping Crease

The popping crease, which is the back edge of the crease marking, shall be in front of and parallel with the bowling crease. It shall have the back edge of the crease marking 4ft./1.22m. from the centre of the stumps and shall extend to a minimum of 6ft./1.83m. on either side of the line of the wicket. The popping crease shall be considered to be unlimited in length.

3. The Return Crease

The return crease marking, of which the inside edge is the crease, shall be at each end of the bowling crease and at right angles to it. The return crease shall be marked to a minimum of 4ft./1.22 m. behind the wicket and shall be considered to be unlimited in length. A forward extension shall be marked to the popping crease.

LAW 10   ROLLING, SWEEPING, MOWING, WATERING THE PITCH AND RE-MARKING OF CREASES

1. Rolling

During the match the pitch may be rolled at the request of the Captain of the batting side, for a period of not more than 7 minutes before the start of each innings, other than the first innings of the match, and before the start of each days play. In addition, if, after the toss and before the first innings of the match, the start is delayed, the Captain of the batting side may request to have the pitch rolled for not more than 7 minutes. However, if in the opinion of the Umpires, the delay has had no significant effect upon the state of the pitch, they shall refuse any request for the rolling of the pitch.

The pitch shall not otherwise be rolled during the match.

The 7 minutes rolling permitted before the start of a day's play shall take place not earlier than half an hour before the start of play and the Captain of the batting side may delay such rolling until 10 minutes before the start of play should he so desire.

If a Captain declares an innings closed less than 15 minutes before the resumption of play, and the other Captain is thereby prevented from exercising his option of 7 minutes rolling or if he is so prevented for any other reason the time for rolling shall be taken out of the normal playing time.

2. Sweeping

Such sweeping of the pitch as is necessary during the match shall be done so that the 7 minutes allowed for rolling the pitch provided for in 1 above is not affected.

3. Mowing

(a) **Responsibilities of Ground Authority and of Umpires**

All mowing which are carried out before the toss for innings shall be the responsibility of the Ground Authority. Thereafter they shall be carried out under the supervision of the Umpires, see Law 7.2 (Selection and Preparation).

(b) **Initial Mowing**

The pitch shall be mown before play begins on the day the match is scheduled to start or in the case of a delayed start on the day the match is expected to start. See 3 (a) above. (Responsibilities of Ground Authority and of Umpires).

(c) **Subsequent Mowing in a Match of 2 or More Days'
Duration**

In a match of two or more days' duration, the pitch shall be
mown daily before play begins. Should this mowing not
take place because of weather conditions, rest days or other
reasons the pitch shall be mown on the first day on which
the match is resumed.

(d) **Mowing of the Outfield in a Match of 2 or More Days'
Duration**

In order to ensure that conditions are as similar as possible
for both sides, the outfield shall normally be mown before
the commencement of play on each day of the match, if
ground and weather conditions allow. See Note (b) to this
Law.

4. Watering

The pitch shall not be watered during a match.

5. Re-Marking Creases

Whenever possible the creases shall be re-marked.

6. Maintenance of Foot Holes

In wet weather, the Umpires shall ensure that the holes made by
the Bowlers and Batsmen are cleaned out and dried whenever
necessary to facilitate play. In matches of 2 or more days' duration,
the Umpires shall allow, if necessary, the re-turfing of foot holes
made by the Bowler in his delivery stride, or the use of quick-
setting fillings for the same purpose, before the start of each day's
play.

7. Securing of Footholds and Maintenance of Pitch

During play, the Umpires shall allow either Batsman to beat the
pitch with his bat and players to secure their footholds by the use
of sawdust, provided that no damage to the pitch is so caused, and
Law 42. (Unfair Play) is not contravened.

NOTES

(a) Non-Turf Pitches

The above Law 10 applies to turf pitches.

The game is played on non-turf pitches in many countries at various levels. Whilst the conduct of the game on these surfaces should always be in accordance with the Laws of Cricket, it is recognised that it may sometimes be necessary for Governing Bodies to lay down special playing conditions to suit the type of non-turf pitch used in their country.

In matches played against touring Teams, any special playing conditions should be agreed in advance by both parties.

(b) Mowing of the Outfield in a Match of 2 or More Days' Duration

If, for reasons other than ground and weather conditions, daily and complete mowing is not possible, the Ground Authority shall notify the Captains and Umpires, before the toss of innings, of the procedure to be adopted for such mowing during the match.

(c) Choice of Rollers

If there is more than one roller available the Captain of the batting side shall have a choice

LAW 11   COVERING THE PITCH

1. Before the Start of a Match

Before the start of a match complete covering of the pitch shall be allowed.

2. During a Match

The pitch shall not be completely covered during a match unless prior arrangement or regulations so provide.

3. Covering Bowlers' Run-Up

Whenever possible, the Bowlers' run-up shall be covered, but the cover so used shall not extend further than 4ft./1.22 m. in front of the popping crease.

NOTES

(a) Removal of Covers

The covers should be removed as promptly as possible whenever the weather permits.

LAW 12   INNINGS

1. Number of Innings
A match shall be of one or two innings of each side according to agreement reached before the start of play.

2. Alternate Innings
In a two innings match each side shall take their innings alternately except in the case provided for in Law 13. (The Follow-On).

3. The Toss
The Captains shall toss for the choice of innings on the filed of play not later than 15 minutes before the time scheduled for the match to start, or before the time agreed upon for play to start.

4. Choice of Innings
The winner of the toss shall notify his decision to bat or to field to the opposing Captain not later than 10 minutes before the time scheduled for the match to start, or before the time agreed upon for play to start. The decision shall not thereafter be altered.

5. Continuation After One Innings of Each Side
Despite the terms of 1. above, in a one innings match, when a result has been reached on the first innings the Captains may agree to the continuation of play if, in their opinion, there is a prospect of carrying the game to a further issue in the time left. See Law 21: (Result).
NOTES
   (a) Limited Innings-One Innings Match
   In a one innings match, each innings may, be agreement, be limited by a number of overs or by a period of time.
   (b) Limited Innings-Two Innings Match
   In a two innings match, the first innings of each side may, by agreement, be limited to a number of overs or by a a period of time.

LAW 13   THE FOLLOW-ON

1. Lead on First Innings
In a two innings match the side which bats first and leads by 200 runs in a match of five days or more, by 150 runs in a three-day or four-day match, by 100 runs in a two-day match, or by 75 runs in a one-day match, shall have the option of requiring the other side to follow their innings.

2. Day's Play Lost
If no play takes place on the first day of a match of 2 or more days' duration, 1 above shall apply in accordance with the number of days' play remaining from the actual start of the match.

LAW 14   DECLARATIONS

1. Time of Declaration
The Captain of the batting side may declare an innings closed at any time during a match irrespective of its duration.

2. Forfeiture of Second Innings
A Captain may forfeit his second innings, provided his decision to do so is notified to the opposing Captain and Umpires in sufficient time to allow 7 minutes rolling of the pitch. See Law 10: (Rolling, Sweeping, Mowing, Watering the Pitch and Re-Marking of Creases). The normal 10 minute interval between innings shall be applied.

LAW 15   START OF PLAY

1. Call of Play
At the start of each innings and of each day's play and on the resumption of play after any interval or interruption the Umpire at the Bowlers' end shall call "play".

2. Practice on the Field
At no time on any day of the match shall there be any bowling or batting practice on the pitch.
No practice may take place on the field if, in the opinion of the Umpires, it could result in a waste of time.

3. Trial Run-Up

No Bowler shall have a trial run-up after "play" has been called in any session of play, except at the fall of a wicket when an Umpire may allow such a trial run-up if he is satisfied that it will not cause any waste of time.

LAW 16   INTERVALS

1. Length

The Umpire shall allow such intervals as have been agreed upon for meals, and 10 minutes between each innings.

2. Luncheon Interval-Innings Ending or Stoppage within 10 Minutes of Interval

If an innings ends or there is a stoppage caused by weather or bad light within 10 minutes of the agreed time for the luncheon interval, the interval shall be taken immediately.

The time remaining in the session of play shall be added to the agreed length of the interval but no extra allowance shall be made for the 10 minutes interval between innings.

3. Tea Interval - Innings Ending or Stoppage within 30 Minutes of Interval

If an innings ends or there is a stoppage caused by weather or bad light within 30 minutes of the agreed time for the tea interval, the interval shall be taken immediately.

The interval shall be of the agreed length and, if applicable, shall include the 10 minute interval between innings.

4. Tea Interval - Continuation of Play

If at the agreed time for the tea interval, nine wickets are down, play shall continue for a period not exceeding 30 minutes or until the innings is concluded.

5. Tea Interval - Agreement to Forego

At any time during the match, the Captains may agree to forego a tea interval.

6. Intervals for Drinks

If both Captains agree before the start of a match that intervals for drinks may be taken, the option to take such intervals shall be available to either side. These intervals shall be restricted to one per session, shall be kept as short as possible, shall not be taken in the last hour of the match and in any case shall not exceed 5 minutes.

The agreed times for these intervals shall be strictly adhered to except that if a wicket falls within 5 minutes of the agreed time then drinks shall be taken out immediately.

If an innings ends or there is a stoppage caused by weather or bad light within 30 minutes of the agreed time for a drinks interval, there will be no interval for drinks in that session.

At any time during the match the Captains may agree to forego any such drinks intervals.

NOTES

(a) Tea Interval-One Day Match

In a one-day match, a specific time for the tea interval need not necessarily be arranged, and it may be agreed to take this interval between the innings of a one-innings match.

(b) Changing the Agreed Time of Intervals

In the event of the ground, weather or light conditions causing a suspension of play, the Umpires, after consultation with the Captains, may decide in the interests of time-saving, to bring forward the time of the luncheon or tea interval.

LAW 17   CESSATION OF PLAY

1. Call of Time

The Umpire at the Bowler's end shall call "time" on the cessation of play before any interval or interruption of play, at the end of each day's play, and at the conclusion of the match. See Law 27: (Appeals).

2. Removal of Bails

After the call of "time", the Umpires shall remove the bails from both wickets.

3. Starting a Last Over

The last over before an interval or the close of play shall be started provided the Umpire, after walking at his normal pace, has arrived at his position behind the stumps at the Bowler's end before time has been reached.

4. Completion of the Last Over of a Session

The last over before an interval or the close of play shall be completed unless a Batsman is out or retires during that over within 2 minutes of the interval or the close of play or unless the Players have occasion to leave the field.

5. Completion of the Last Over of a Match

An over in progress at the close of play on the final day of a match shall be completed at the request of either Captain even if a wicket falls after time has been reached.

If during the last over the Players have occasion to leave the field the Umpires shall call "time" and there shall be no resumption of play and the match shall be at an end.

6. Last Hour of Match - Number of Overs

The Umpires shall indicate when one hour of playing time of the match remains according to the agreed hours of play. The next over after that moment shall be the first of a minimum of 20 6-ball overs, (15 8-ball overs), provided a result is not reached earlier or there is no interval or interruption of play.

7. Last Hour of Match - Intervals Between Innings and Interruptions of Play

If, at the commencement of the last hour of the match, an interval or interruption of play is in progress or if, during the last hour there is an interval between innings or an interruption of play, the minimum number of overs to be bowled on the resumption of play shall be reduced in proportion to the duration within the last hour of the match, of any such interval or interruption.

The minimum number of overs to be bowled after a resumption of play shall be calculated as follows:

(a) In the case of an interval or interruption of play being in progress at the commencement of the last hour of the match, or in the case of a first interval or interruption a deduction shall be made from the minimum of 20 6-ball overs (or 15 8-ball overs).

(b) If there is a later interval or interruption a further deduction shall be made from the minimum number of overs which should have been bowled following the last resumption of play.

(c) These deductions shall be based on the following factors:

(i) the number of overs already bowled in the last hour of the match or, in the case of a later interval or interruption in the last session of play.

(ii) the number of overs lost as a result of the interval or interruption allowing one 6-ball over for every full three minutes (or one 8-ball over for every full four minutes) of interval or interruption.

(iii) any over left uncompleted at the end of an innings to be excluded from these calculations.

(iv) any over of the minimum number to be played which is left uncompleted at the start of an interruption of play shall be completed when play is resumed and to count as one over bowled.

(v) an interval to start with the end of an innings and to end 10 minutes later; an interruption to start on the call of "time" and to end on the call of "play".

(d) In the event of an innings being completed and a new innings commencing during the last hour of the match, the number of overs to be bowled in the new innings shall be calculated on the basis of one 6-ball over for every three minutes or part thereof remaining for play (or one 8-ball over for every four minutes or part thereof remaining for play); or alternatively on the basis that sufficient overs be bowled to enable the full minimum quota of overs to be completed un circumstances governed by (a), (b) and (c) above. In all such cases the alternative which allows the greater number of overs shall be employed.

8. Bowler Unable to Complete an Over During Last Hour of the Match

If, for any reason, a Bowler is unable to complete an over during the period of play referred to in 6 above, Law 22.7: (Bowler Incapacitated or Suspended during an Over) shall apply.

LAW 18   SCORING

1. A Run

The score shall be reckoned by runs. A run is scored:-

(a) So often as the Batsmen, after a hit or at any time while the ball is in play, shall have crossed and made good their ground from end to end.

(b) When a boundary is scored. See Law 19: (Boundaries).

(c) When penalty runs are awarded. See 6 below.

2. Short Runs

(a) If either Batsman runs a short run, the Umpire shall call and signal "one short" as soon as the ball becomes dead and that run shall not be scored. A run is short if a Batsman fails to make good his ground on turning for a further run.

(b) Although a short run shortens the succeeding one, the latter, if completed shall count.

(c) If either or both Batsmen deliberately run short the Umpire shall, as soon as he sees that the fielding side have no chance of dismissing either Batsman, call and signal "dead ball" and disallow any runs attempted or previously scored. The Batsmen shall return to their original ends.

(d) If both Batsmen run short in one and the same run, only one run shall be deducted.

(e) Only if three or more runs are attempted can more than one be short and then, subject to (c) and (d) above, all runs so called shall be disallowed. If there has been more than one short run the Umpires shall instruct the Scorers as to the number of runs disallowed.

3. Striker Caught

If the Striker is Caught, no run shall be scored.

4. Batsman Run Out

If a Batsman is Run Out, only that run which was being attempted shall not be scored. If, however, an injured Striker himself is run out no runs shall be scored. See Law 2.7. (Transgression of the Laws by an Injured Batsman or Runner).

5. Batsman Obstructing the Field

If a Batsman is out Obstructing the Field, any runs completed before the obstruction occurs shall be scored unless such obstruction prevents a catch being made in which case no runs shall be scored.

6. Runs Scored for Penalties

Runs shall be scored for penalties under Laws 20: (Lost Ball), 24: (No Ball), 25: (Wide Ball), 41.1: (Fielding the Ball) and for boundary allowances under Law 19: (Boundaries).

7. Batsman Returning to Wicket he has Left

If, while the ball is in play, the Batsmen have crossed in running, neither shall return to the wicket he has left even though a short run has been called or no run has been scored as in the case of a catch. Batsmen, however, shall return to the wickets they originally left in the cases of a boundary and of any disallowance of runs and of an injured Batsman being, himself, run out. See Law 2.7: (Transgression of the Laws by an Injured Batsman or Runner).

NOTES

(a) Short Run

A Striker taking stance in front of his popping crease may run from that point without penalty.

LAW 19   BOUNDARIES

1. The Boundary of the Playing Area

Before the toss for innings, the Umpires shall agree with both Captains on the boundary of the playing area. The boundary shall, if possible, be marked by a white line, a rope laid on the ground, or a fence. If flags or posts only are used to mark a boundary, the imaginary line joining such points shall be regarded as the boundary. An obstacle, or person, within the playing area shall not be regarded as a boundary unless so decided by the Umpires before the toss of innings. Sight-screens within, or partially within, the playing area shall be regarded as the boundary and when the ball strikes or passes within or under or directly over any part of the screen, a boundary shall be scored.

2. Runs Scored for Boundaries

Before the toss of innings, the Umpires shall agree with both Captains the runs to be allowed for boundaries, and in deciding the allowance for them, the Umpires and Captains shall be guided by the prevailing custom of the ground. The allowance for a boundary shall normally be 4 runs, and 6 runs for all hits pitching over and clear of the boundary line or fence, even though the ball has been previously touched by a Fieldsman. 6 runs shall also be scored if a Fieldsman, after catching a ball, carries it over the boundary. See Law 32: (Caught) Note (a). 6 runs shall not be scored when a ball struck by the Striker hits a sightscreen full pitch if the screen is within, or partially within, the playing area, but if the ball is struck directly over a sightscreen so situated, 6 runs shall be scored.

3. A Boundary

A boundary shall be scored and signalled by the Umpire at the Bowler's end whenever, in his opinion:-

(a) A ball in play touches or crosses the boundary, however marked.

(b) A Fieldsman with ball in hand touches or grounds any part of his person on or over a boundary line.

(c) A Fieldsman with ball in hand grounds any part of his person over a boundary fence or board. This allows the Fieldsman to touch or lean on or over a boundary fence or board in preventing a boundary.

4. Runs Exceeding Boundary Allowance

The runs completed at the instant the ball reaches the boundary shall count if they exceed the boundary allowance.

5. Overthrows or Wilful Act of a Fieldsman

If the boundary results from an overthrow or from the wilful act of a Fieldsman, any runs already completed and the allowance shall be added to the score. The run in progress shall count provided that the Batsmen have crossed at the instant of the throw or act.

NOTES

(a) Position of Sight-Screens

Sight-Screens should, if possible, be positioned wholly outside the playing area, as near as possible to the boundary line.

LAW 20   LOST BALL

1. Runs Scored

If a ball in play cannot be found or recovered any fieldsman may call "lost ball" when 6 runs shall be added to the score; but if more than 6 have been run before "lost ball" is called, as many runs as have been completed shall be scored. The run in progress shall count provided that the Batsmen have crossed at the instant of the call of "lost ball".

2. How Scored

The runs shall be added to the score of the Striker if the ball has been struck, but otherwise to the score of byes, leg-byes, no-balls or wides as the case may be.

LAW 21   THE RESULT

1. A Win - Two Innings Matches

The side which has scored a total of runs in excess of that scored by the opposing side in its two completed innings shall be the winners.

2. A Win - One Innings Matches

(a) One innings matches, unless played out as in 1. above, shall be decided on the first innings, but see Law 12.5: (Continuation After One Innings of Each Side).

(b) If the Captains agree to continue play after the completion of one innings of each side in accordance with Law 12.5: (Continuation After One Innings of Each Side) and a result is not achieved on the second innings, the first innings result shall stand.

3. Umpires Awarding a Match

(a) A Match shall be lost by a side which, during the match,
   (i) refuses to play, or
   (ii) concedes defeat,
and the Umpires shall award the match to the other side.

(b) Should both batsmen at the wickets or the fielding side leave the field at any time without the agreement of the Umpires, this shall constitute a refusal to play and, on appeal, the Umpires shall award the match to the other side in accordance with (a) above.

4. A Tie

The result of a match shall be a tie when the scores are equal at the conclusion of play, but only if the side batting last has completed its innings.

If the scores of the completed first innings of a one-day match are equal, it shall be a tie but only if the match has not been played out to a further conclusion.

5. A Draw

A match not determined in any of the ways as in 1, 2, 3 and 4 above shall count as a draw.

6. Correctness of Result

Any decision as to the correctness of the scores shall be the responsibility of the Umpires. See Law 3.14: (Correctness of Scores).

If, after the Umpires and Players have left the field, in the belief that the match has been concluded, the Umpires decide that the mistake in scoring has occurred, which affects the result, and provided time has not been reached, they shall order play to resume and to continue until the agreed finishing time unless a result is reached earlier.

If the Umpires decide that a mistake has occurred and time has been reached, the Umpires shall immediately inform both Captains of the necessary corrections to the scores and, if applicable, to the result.

7. Acceptance of Result

In accepting the scores as notified by the scorers and agreed by the Umpires, the Captains of both sides thereby accept the result.

NOTES

(a) Statement of Results

The result of a finished match is stated as a win by runs, except in the case of a win by the side batting last when it is by the number of wickets still then to fall.

(b) Winning Hit or Extras

As soon as the side has won, see 1. and 2. above, the Umpire shall call "time", the match is finished, and nothing that happens thereafter other than as a result of a mistake in scoring, see 6. above, shall be regarded as part of the match. However, if a boundary constitutes the winning hit—or extras— and the boundary allowance exceeds the number of runs required to win the match, such runs scored shall be credited to the side's total and, in the case of a hit to the Striker's score.

LAW 22   THE OVER

1. Number of Balls

The ball shall be bowled from each wicket alternately in overs of either 6 or 8 balls according to agreement before the match.

2. Call of "Over"

When the agreed number of balls has been bowled, and as the ball becomes dead or when it becomes clear to the Umpire at the Bowler's end that both the fielding side and the Batsmen at the wicket have ceased to regard the ball as in play, the Umpire shall call "over" before leaving the wicket.

3. No Ball or Wide Ball

Neither a no ball nor a wide ball shall be reckoned as one of the over.

4. Umpire Miscounting

If an Umpire miscounts the number of balls, the over as counted by the Umpire shall stand.

5. Bowler Changing Ends

A Bowler shall be allowed to change ends as often as desired provided only that he does not bowl two overs consecutively in an innings.

6. The Bowler Finishing an Over

A Bowler shall finish an over in progress unless he be incapacitated or be suspended under Law 42.8: (The Bowling of Fast Short Pitched Balls), 42.9: (The Bowling of Fast High Full Pitches), 42.10: (Time Wasting) and 42.11: (Players Damaging the Pitch). If an over is left incomplete for any reason at the start of an interval or interruption of play, it shall be finished on the resumption of play.

7. Bowler Incapacitated or Suspended During an Over

If, for any reason, a Bowler is incapacitated while running up to bowl the first ball of an over, or is incapacitated or suspended during an over, the Umpire shall call and signal "dead ball" and another Bowler shall be allowed to bowl or complete the over from the same end, provided only that he shall not bowl two overs, or part thereof, consecutively in one innings.

8. Position of Non-Striker

The Batsman at the Bowler's end shall normally stand on the opposite side of the wicket to that from which the ball is being delivered, unless a request to do otherwise is granted by the Umpire.

LAW 23   DEAD BALL

1. The Ball Becomes Dead, when:

(a) It is finally settled in the hands of the Wicket Keeper or the Bowler.

(b) It reaches or pitches over the boundary.

(c) A Batsman is out.

(d) Whether played or not, it lodges in the clothing or equipment of a Batsman or the clothing of an Umpire.

(e) A ball lodges in a protective helmet worn by a member of the fielding side.

(f) A penalty is awarded under Law 20: (Lost Ball) or Law 41.1: (Fielding the Ball).

(g) The Umpire calls "over" or "time".

2. Either Umpire Shall Call and Signal "Dead Ball", when:

(a) He intervenes in a case of unfair play.

(b) A serious injury to a Player or Umpire occurs.

(c) He is satisfied that, for an adequate reason, the Striker is not ready to receive the ball and makes no attempt to play it.

(d) The Bowler drops the ball accidentally before delivery, or the ball does not leave his hand for any reason, other than in an attempt to run out the Non-Striker, (See Law 24.5—Bowler Attempting to Run Out Non-Striker Before Delivery).

(e) One or both bails fall from the Striker's wicket before he receives delivery.

(f) He leaves his normal position for consultation.

(g) He is required to do so under Law 26.3: (Disallowance of Leg-Byes), etc.

3. The Ball Ceases to be Dead, when:

(a) The Bowler starts his run up or bowling action.

4. The Ball is Not Dead, when:

(a) It strikes an Umpire (unless it lodges in his dress).

(b) The wicket is broken or struck down (unless a Batsman is out thereby).

(c) An unsuccessful appeal is made.

(d) The wicket is broken accidentally either by the Bowler during his delivery or by a Batsman in running.

(e) The Umpire has called "no ball" or "wide".

NOTES

(a) Ball Finally Settled

Whether the ball is finally settled or not —see 1 (a) above— must be a question for the Umpires alone to decide.

(b) Action on Call of "Dead Ball"

(i) *If "dead ball" is called prior to the Striker receiving a delivery the Bowler shall be allowed an additional ball.*

(ii) *If "dead ball" is called after the Striker receives a delivery the Bowler shall not be allowed an additional ball, unless a "no ball" or "wide" has been called.*

LAW 24   NO BALL

1. Mode of Delivery

The Umpire shall indicate to the Striker whether the Bowler intends to bowl over or round the wicket, overarm or underarm, or right or left-handed. Failure on the part of the Bowler to indicate in advance a change in his mode of delivery is unfair and the Umpire shall call and signal "no ball".

2. Fair Delivery - The Arm

For a delivery to be fair the ball must be bowled not thrown—see Note (a) below. If either Umpire is not entirely satisfied with the absolute fairness of a delivery in this respect he shall call and signal "no ball" instantly upon delivery.

3. Fair Delivery - The Feet

The Umpire at the bowler's wicket shall call and signal "no ball" if he is not satisfied that in the delivery stride:

(a) the Bowler's back foot has landed within and not touching the return crease or its forward extension

or

(b) some part of the front foot whether grounded or raised was behind the popping crease.

4. Bowler Throwing at Striker's Wicket Before Delivery

If the Bowler, before delivering the ball, throws it at the Striker's wicket in an attempt to run him out, the Umpire shall call and signal "no ball". See Law 42.12: (Batsman Unfairly stealing a Run) and Law 38: (Run Out).

5. Bowler Attempting to Run Out Non-Striker Before Delivery

If the Bowler, before delivering the ball, attempts to run out the non-Striker, any runs which result shall be allowed and shall be scored as no balls. Such an attempt shall not count as a ball in the over. The Umpire shall not call "no ball". See Law 42.12: (Batsman Unfairly Stealing a Run).

6. Infringement of Laws by a Wicket-Keeper or a Fieldsman

The Umpire shall call and signal "no ball" in the event of the Wicket-Keeper infringing Law 40.1: (Position of Wicket-Keeper) or a Fieldsman infringing Law 41.2: (Limitation of On-Side Fieldsmen) or Law 41.3: (Position of Fieldsmen).

7. Revoking a Call

An Umpire shall revoke the call "no ball" if the ball does not leave the Bowler's hand for any reason. See Law 23.2: (Either Umpire Shall Call and Signal "Dead Ball").

8. Penalty

A penalty of one run for a no ball shall be scored if no runs are made otherwise.

9. Runs From a No Ball

The Striker may hit a no ball and whatever runs result shall be added to his score. Runs made otherwise from a no ball shall be scored no balls.

10. Out From a No Ball

The Striker shall be out from a no ball if he breaks Law 34: (Hit the Ball Twice) and either Batsman may be Run Out or shall be given out if either breaks Law 33: (Handled the Ball) or Law 37: (Obstructing the Field).

11. Batsman Given Out Off a No Ball

Should a Batsman be given out off a no ball the penalty for bowling it shall stand unless runs are otherwise scored.
NOTES
(a) Definition of a Throw

A ball shall be deemed to have been thrown if, in the opinion of either Umpire, the process of straightening the bowling arm, whether it be partial or complete, takes place during that part of the delivery swing which directly precedes the ball leaving the hand. This definition shall not debar a Bowler from the use of the wrist in the delivery swing.
(b) No Ball not Counting in Over

A no ball shall not be reckoned as one of the over. See Law 22.3: (No Ball or Wide Ball).

LAW 25   WIDE BALL

1. Judging a Wide

If the Bowler bowls the ball so high over or so wide of the wicket that, in the opinion of the Umpire it passes out of reach of the Striker, standing in a normal guard position, the Umpire shall call and signal "wide ball" as soon as it has passed the line of the Striker's wicket.

The Umpire shall not adjudge a ball as being a wide if:

(a) The Striker, by moving from his guard position, causes the ball to pass out of his reach.

(b) The striker moves and thus brings the ball within his reach.

2. Penalty

A penalty of one run for a wide shall be scored if no runs are made otherwise.

3. Ball Coming to Rest in Front of the Striker

If a ball which the Umpire considers to have been delivered comes to rest in front of the line of the Striker's wicket, "wide" shall not be called. The Striker has a right, without interference from the fielding side, to make one attempt to hit the ball. If the fielding side interfere, the Umpire shall replace the ball where it came to rest and shall order the Fieldsmen to resume the places they occupied in the field before the ball was delivered.

The Umpire shall call and signal "dead ball" as soon as it is clear that the Striker does not intend to hit the ball, or after the Striker has made one unsuccessful attempt to hit the ball.

4. Revoking a Call

The Umpire shall revoke the call if the Striker hits a ball which has been called "wide".

5. Ball Not Dead

The ball does not become dead on the call of "wide ball"—see Law 23.4: (The Ball is Not Dead).

6. Runs Resulting from a Wide

All runs which are run or result from a wide ball which is not a no ball shall be scored wide balls, or if no runs are made one shall be scored.

7. Out from a Wide

The Striker shall be out from a wide ball if he breaks Law 35: (Hit wicket) or Law 39: (Stumped). Either Batsman may be Run Out and shall be out if he breaks Law 33: (Handled the Ball) or Law 37: (Obstructing the Field).

8. Batsman Given Out Off a Wide

Should a Batsman be given out off a wide, the penalty for bowling it shall stand unless runs are otherwise made.
NOTES
   (a) Wide Ball not Counting in Over
   A wide ball shall not be reckoned as one of the over—see Law 22.3: (No Ball or Wide Ball).

LAW 26   BYE AND LEG-BYE

1. Byes

If the ball, not having been called "wide" or "no ball" passes the Striker without touching his bat or person, and any runs are obtained, the Umpire shall signal "bye" and the run or runs shall be credited as such to the batting side.

2. Leg-Byes

If the ball, not having been called "wide" or "no ball" is unintentionally deflected by the Striker's dress or person, except a hand holding the bat, and any runs are obtained the Umpire shall signal "leg-bye"and the run or runs so scored shall be credited as such to the batting side.

Such leg-byes shall only be scored if, in the opinion of the Umpire, the Striker has:
   (a) attempted to play the ball with his bat, or
   (b) tried to avoid being hit by the ball.

3. Disallowance of Leg-Byes

In the case of a deflection by the Striker's person, other than in 2 (a) and (b) above, the Umpire shall call and signal "dead ball" as soon as one run has been completed or when it is clear that a run is not being attempted or the ball has reached the boundary.

On the call and signal of "dead ball" the Batsmen shall return to their original ends and no runs shall be allowed.

LAW 27   APPEALS

1. Time of Appeals

The Umpires shall not give a Batsman out unless appealed to by the other side which shall be done prior to the Bowler beginning his run-up or bowling action to deliver the next ball. Under Law 23.1: (g) (The Ball becomes Dead) the ball is dead on "over" being called; this does not, however, invalidate an appeal made prior to the first ball of the following over provided "time" has not been called. See Law 17.1: (Call of Time).

2. An Appeal "How's That?"

An appeal "How's That?" shall cover all ways of being out.

3. Answering Appeals

The Umpire at the Bowler's wicket shall answer appeals before the other Umpire in all cases except those arising out of Law 35: (Hit Wicket) or Law 39: (Stumped) or Law 38: (Run Out) when this occurs at the Striker's wicket.

Umpire shall, within his jurisdiction, answer the appeal or a further appeal, provided it is made in time in accordance with 1. above (Time of Appeals).

4. Consultation by Umpires

An Umpire may consult with the other Umpire on a point of fact which the latter may have been in a better position to see and shall then give his decision. If, after consultation, there is still doubt remaining the decision shall be in favour of the Batsman.

5. Batsman Leaving his Wicket under a Misapprehension

The Umpires shall intervene if satisfied that a Batsman, not having been given out, has left his wicket under a misapprehension that he has been dismissed.

6. Umpire's Decision

The Umpire's decision is final. He may alter his decision, provided that such alteration is made promptly.

7. Withdrawal of an Appeal

In exceptional circumstances the Captain of the fielding side may seek permission of the Umpire to withdraw an appeal providing the outgoing Batsman has not left the playing area. If this is allowed, the Umpire shall cancel his decision.

LAW 28   THE WICKET IS DOWN

1. Wicket Down

The wicket is down if:

(a) Either the ball or the Striker's bat or person completely removes either bail from the top of the stumps. A disturbance of a bail, whether temporary or not, shall not constitute a complete removal, but the wicket is down if a bail in falling lodges between two of the stumps.

(b) Any player completely removes with his hand or arm a bail from the top of the stumps, providing that the ball is held in that hand or in the hand of the arm so used.

(c) When both bails are off, a stump is struck out of the ground by the ball, or a player strikes or pulls a stump out of the ground, providing that the ball is held in the hand(s) or in the hand of the arm so used.

2. One Bail Off

If one bail is off, it shall be sufficient for the purpose of putting the wicket down to remove the remaining bail, or to strike or pull any of the three stumps out of the ground in any of the ways stated in 1. above.

3. All the Stumps Out of the Ground

If all the stumps are out of the ground, the fielding side shall be allowed to put back one or more stumps in order to have an opportunity of putting the wicket down.

4. Dispensing with Bails

If owing to the strength of the wind, it has been agreed to dispense with the bails in accordance with Law 8: Note (a) (Dispensing with Bails) the decision as to when the wicket is down is one for the Umpires to decide on the facts before them. In such circumstances and if the Umpires so decide the wicket shall be held to be down even thought stump has not been struck out of the ground.

NOTES

(a) Remaking the Wicket

If the wicket is broken while the ball is in play, it is not the Umpires duty to remake the wicket until the ball has become dead—see Law 23: (Dead Ball). A member of the fielding side, however, may remake the wicket in such circumstances.

LAW 29   BATSMAN OUT OF HIS GROUND

1. When out of his Ground

A Batsman shall be considered to be out of his ground unless some part of his bat in his hand or of his person is grounded behind the line of the popping crease.

LAW 30   BOWLED

1. Out Bowled

The Striker shall be out bowled if:

(a) His wicket is bowled down, even if the ball first touches his bat or person.

(b) He breaks his wicket by hitting or kicking the ball on to it before the completion of a stroke, or as a result of attempting to guard his wicket. See Law 34.1: (Out-Hit the Ball Twice).

NOTES

(a) Out Bowled-Not L.B.W.

The Striker it out Bowled if the ball is deflected on to his wicket even though a decision against him would be justified under Law 36: (Leg Before Wicket).

LAW 31   TIMED OUT

1. Out Timed Out

An incoming Batsman shall be out Timed Out if he wilfully takes more than two minutes to come in—the two minutes being timed from the moment a wicket falls until the new batsman steps on to the field of play.

If this is not complied with and if the Umpire is satisfied that the delay was wilful and if an appeal is made, the new Batsman shall be given out by the Umpire at the Bowler's end.

2. Time to be Added

The time taken by the Umpires to investigate the cause of the delay shall be added at the normal close of play.

NOTES

(a) Entry in Score Book

The correct entry in the score book when a Batsman is given out under this Law is "timed out", and the Bowler does not get credit for the wicket.

(b) Batsmen Crossing on the Field of Play

It is an essential duty of the Captains to ensure that the in-going Batsman passes the out-going one before the latter leaves the field of play.

LAW 32   CAUGHT

1. Out Caught

The Striker shall be out Caught if the ball touches his bat or if it touches below the wrist his hand or glove, holding the bat, and is subsequently held by a Fieldsman before it touches the ground.

2. A Fair Catch

A Catch shall be considered to have been fairly made if:

(a) The Fieldsman is within the field of play throughout the act of making the catch.

(i) The act of making the catch shall start from the time when the Fieldsman first handles the ball and shall end when he both retains complete control over the further

(ii) In order to be within the field of play, the Fieldsman may not touch or ground any part of his person on or over a boundary line. When the boundary is marked by a fence or board the Fieldsman may not ground any part of his person over the boundary fence or board, but may touch or lean over the boundary fence or board in completing the catch.

(b) The ball is hugged to the body of the catcher or accidentally lodges in his dress or, in the case of the Wicket-Keeper, in his pads. However, a Striker may not be caught if a ball lodges in a protective helmet worn by a Fieldsman, in which case the Umpire shall call and signal "dead ball".

(c) The ball does not touch the ground even though a hand holding it does so in effecting the catch.

(d) A Fieldsman catches the ball, after it has been lawfully played a second time by the Striker, but only if the ball has not touched the ground since being first struck.

(e) A Fieldsman catches the ball after it has touched an Umpire, another Fieldsman or the other Batsman. However, a Striker may not be caught if a ball has touched a protective helmet won by a Fieldsman.

(f) The Ball is caught off an obstruction within the boundary provided it has not previously been agreed to regard the obstruction as a boundary.

3. Scoring of Runs

If a Striker is caught, no runs shall be scored.

NOTES

(a) Scoring from an Attempted Catch

When a Fieldsman carrying the ball touches or grounds any part of his person on or over a boundary marked by a line, 6 runs shall be scored.

(b) Ball Still in Play

If a Fieldsman releases the ball before he crosses the boundary, the ball will be considered to be still in play and in may be caught by another Fieldsman. However, if the original

Fieldsman returns to the field of play and handles the ball, a catch may not be made.

LAW 33   HANDLED THE BALL

1. Out Handled the Ball

Either Batsman on appeal shall be out Handled the Ball if he wilfully touches the ball while in play with the hand not holding the bat unless he does so with the consent of the opposite side.
NOTES
(a) Entry in Score Book
The correct entry in the score book when a Batsman is given out under this Law is "handled the ball", and the Bowler does not get credit for the wicket.

LAW 34   HIT THE BALL TWICE

1. Out Hit the Ball Twice

The Striker, on appeal, shall be out Hit the Ball Twice if, after the ball is struck or is stopped by any part of his person, he wilfully strikes it again with his bat or person except for the sole purpose of guarding his wicket: this he may do with his bat or any part of his person other than his hands, but see Law 37.2: (Obstructing a Ball From Being Caught).

For the purpose of this Law, a hand holding the bat shall be regarded as part of the bat.

2. Returning the Ball to a Fieldsman

The Striker, on appeal, shall be out under this Law, if without the consent of the opposite side, he uses his bat or person to return the ball to any of the fielding side.

3. Runs from Ball Lawfully Struck Twice

No runs except those which result from an overthrow or penalty, see Law 41: (the Fieldsman), shall be scored from a ball lawfully struck twice.
NOTES
(a) Entry in Score Book

The correct entry in the score book when the Striker is given out under this Law is "hit the ball twice", and the Bowler does not get credit for the wicket.

(b) Runs Credited to the Batsman

Any runs awarded under 3. above as a result of an overthrow or penalty shall be credited to the Striker, provided the ball in the first instance has touched the bat, or, if otherwise as extras.

LAW 35   HIT WICKET

1. Out Hit Wicket

The Striker shall be out Hit Wicket if, while the ball is in play:

(a) His wicket is broken with any part of his person, dress, or equipment as a result of any action taken by him in preparing to receive or in receiving a delivery, or in setting off for his first run, immediately after playing, or playing at, the ball.

(b) He hits down his wicket whilst lawfully making a second stroke for the purpose of guarding his wicket within the provisions of Law 34.1: (Out Hit the Ball Twice).

NOTES

(a) Not Out Hit Wicket

A Batsman is not out under this Law should his wicket be broken in any of the ways referred to in 1 (a) above if:

(i) It occurs while he is in the act of running, other than in setting off for his first run immediately after playing at the ball, or while he is avoiding being run out or stumped.

(ii) The Bowler after starting his run-up or bowling action does not deliver the ball; in which case the Umpire shall immediately call and signal "dead ball".

(iii) It occurs whilst he is avoiding a throw-in at any time.

LAW 36   LEG BEFORE WICKET

1. Out L.B.W.

The Striker shall be out L.B.W. in the circumstances set out below:

(a) **Striker Attempting to Play the Ball**

The Striker shall be out L.B.W. if he first intercepts with any part of his person, dress or equipment a fair ball which would have hit the wicket and which has not previously touched his bat or a hand holding the bat, provide that:

(i) The ball pitched, in a straight line between wicket and wicket or on the off side of the Striker's wicket, or was intercepted full pitch

and

(ii) the point of impact is in a straight line between wicket and wicket, even if above the level of the bails.

(b) **Striker Making No Attempt to Play the Ball**

The Striker shall be out L.B.W. even if the ball is intercepted outside the line of the off-stump, if, in the opinion of the Umpire, he has made no genuine attempt to play the ball with his bat, but has intercepted the ball with some part of his person and if the other circumstances set out in (a) above apply.

LAW 37   OBSTRUCTING THE FIELD

1. Wilful Obstruction

Either Batsman, on appeal, shall be out Obstructing the Field if he wilfully obstructs the opposite side by word or action.

2. Obstructing a Ball from Being Caught

The Striker, on appeal, shall be out should wilful obstruction by either Batsman prevent a catch being made.

This shall apply even though the Striker causes the obstruction in lawfully guarding his wicket under the provisions of Law 34. See Law 34.1: (Out Hit the Ball Twice).

NOTES

(a) Accidental Obstruction

The Umpires must decide whether the obstruction was wilful or not. The accidental interception of a throw-in by a Batsman while running does not break this Law.

(b) Entry in Score Book

The correct entry in the score book when a Batsman is given out under this Law is "obstructing the field", and the bowler does not get credit for the wicket.

LAW 38   RUN OUT

1. Out Run Out

Either Batsman shall be out Run Out if in running or at any time while the ball is in play—except in the circumstances described in Law 39: (Stumped)—he is out of his ground and his wicket is put down by the opposite side. If, however, a Batsman in running makes good his ground he shall not be out Run Out, if he subsequently leaves his ground, in order to avoid injury, and the wicket is put down.

2. "No Ball" Called

If a no ball has been called, the Striker shall not be given Run Out unless he attempts to run.

3. Which Batsman is Out

If the Batsmen have crossed in running, he who runs for the wicket which is put down shall be out; if they have not crossed, he who has left the wicket which is put down shall be out. If a Batsman remains in his ground or returns to his ground and the other Batsman joins him there, the latter shall be out if his wicket is put down.

4. Scoring of Runs

If a Batsman is run out, only that run which is being attempted shall not be scored. If however, an injured Striker himself is run out, no runs shall be scored. See Law 2.7: (Transgression of the Laws by an Injured Batsman or Runner).

NOTES

(a) Ball Played on to Opposite Wicket

If the ball is played on to the opposite wicket neither Batsman is liable to be Run Out unless the ball has been touched by a Fieldsman before the wicket is broken.

(b) Entry in Score Book

The correct entry in the score book when the Striker is given

out under this Law is "run out", and the Bowler does not get credit for the wicket..
(c) Run Out off a Fieldsman"s Helmet.
If, having been played by a Batsman, or having come off his person, the ball rebounds directly from a Fieldsman's helmet on to the stumps, with either Batsman out of his ground, the Batsman shall be "Not Out".

LAW 39   STUMPED

1. Out Stumped
The Striker shall be out Stumped if, in receiving the ball, not being a no-ball, he is out of his ground otherwise than in attempting a run and the wicket is put down by the Wicket-Keeper without the intervention of another Fieldsman.

2. Action by the Wicket-Keeper
The Wicket-Keeper may take the ball in front of the wicket in an attempt to Stump the Striker only if the ball has touched the bat or person of the Striker.
NOTES
(a) Ball Rebounding from Wicket-Keeper's Person
The Striker may be out Stumped if in the circumstances stated in 1. above, the wicket is broken by a ball rebounding from the Wicket-Keeper's person or equipment other than a protective helmet or is kicked or thrown by the Wicket-Keeper on to the wicket.

LAW 40   THE WICKET-KEEPER

1. Position of Wicket-Keeper
The Wicket-Keeper shall remain wholly behind the wicket until a ball delivered by the Bowler touches the bat or person of the Striker, or passes the wicket, or until the Striker attempts a run. In the event of the Wicket-Keeper contravening this Law, the Umpire at the Striker's end shall call and signal "no ball" at the instant of delivery or as soon as possible thereafter.

2. Restriction on Actions of the Wicket-Keeper

If the Wicket-Keeper interferes with the Striker's right to play the ball and to guard his wicket, the Striker shall not be out, except under Law 33: (Handled the Ball), 34: (Hit the Ball Twice), 37: (Obstructing the Field) and 38: (Run Out).

3. Interference with the Wicket-Keeper by the Striker

If in the legitimate defence of his wicket, the Striker interferes with the Wicket-Keeper, he shall not be out, except as provided for in Law 37.2: (Obstructing a Ball from Being Caught).

LAW 41   THE FIELDSMAN

1. Fielding the Ball

The Fieldsman may stop the ball with any part of his person, but if he wilfully stops it otherwise, 5 runs shall be added to the run or runs already scored; if no run has been scored 5 penalty runs shall be awarded. The run in progress shall count provided that the Batsmen have crossed at the instant of the act. If the ball has been struck, the penalty shall be added to the to the score of the Striker, but otherwise to the score of byes, leg-byes, no balls or wides at the case may be.

2. Limitation of On-Side Fieldsmen

The number of on-side Fieldsmen behind the popping crease at the instant of the Bowler's delivery shall not exceed two. In the event of infringement by the fielding side the Umpire at the Striker's end shall call and signal "no ball" at the instant of delivery or as soon as possible thereafter.

3. Position of Fieldsmen

Whilst the ball is in play and until the ball has made contact with the bat or the Striker's person or has passed his bat, no Fieldsman, other than the Bowler, may stand on or have any part of his person extended over the pitch (measuring 22 yards/20.12m x 10ft. 3.05m). In the event of a Fieldsman contravening this Law, the Umpire at the bowler's end shall call and signal "no ball" at the instant of delivery or as soon as possible thereafter. See Law 40.1: (Position of Wicket-Keeper).

4. Fieldsman's Protective Helmets

Protective helmets, when not in use by members of the fielding side, shall only be placed, if above the surface, on the ground behind the Wicket-Keeper. In the event of the ball, when in play, striking a helmet whilst in this position, five penalty runs shall be awarded, as laid down in Law 41.1 and Note (a).

NOTES

(a) Batsmen Changing Ends

The 5 runs referred to in 1. above are a penalty and the Batsmen do not change ends solely by reason of this penalty.

LAW 42   UNFAIR PLAY

1. Responsibility of Captains

The Captains are responsible at all times for ensuring that play is conducted within the spirit of the game as well as within the Laws.

2. Responsibility of Umpires

The Umpires are the sole judges of fair and unfair play.

3. Intervention by the Umpire

The Umpires shall intervene without appeal by calling and signalling "dead ball" in the case of unfair play, but should not otherwise interfere with the progress of the game except as required to do so by the Laws.

4. Lifting the Seam

A Player shall not lift the seam of the ball for any reason. Should this be done, the Umpires shall change the ball for one of similar condition to that in use prior to the contravention. See Note (a).

5. Changing the Condition of the Ball

Any member of the fielding side may polish the ball provided that such polishing wastes no time and that no artificial substance is used. No-one shall rub the ball on the ground or use any artificial substance or take any other action to alter the condition of the ball.

In the event of a contravention of this Law, the Umpires, after consultation, shall change the ball for one of similar condition to that in use prior to the contravention.

This Law does not prevent a member of the fielding side from drying a wet ball, or removing mud from the ball. See Note (b).

6. Incommoding the Striker

An Umpire is justified in intervening under this Law and shall call and signal "dead ball" if, in his opinion, any Player of the fielding side incommodes the Striker by any noise or action while he is receiving a ball.

7. Obstruction of a Batsman in Running

It shall be considered unfair if any Fieldsman wilfully obstructs a Batsman in running. In these circumstances the Umpire shall call and signal "dead ball" and allow any completed runs and the run in progress or alternatively any boundary scored.

8. The Bowling of Fast Short Pitched Balls

The bowling of fast short pitched balls is unfair if, in the opinion of the Umpire at the Bowler's end, it constitutes an attempt to intimidate the Striker. See Note (d).

Umpires shall consider intimidation to be the deliberate bowling of fast short pitched balls which by their length, height and direction are intended or likely to inflict physical injury on the Striker. The relative skill of the Striker shall also be taken into consideration.

In the event of such unfair bowling, the Umpire at the Bowler's end shall adopt the following procedure:

(a) In the first instance the Umpire shall call and signal "no ball", caution the Bowler and inform the other Umpire, the Captain of the fielding side and the Batsmen of what has occurred.

(b) If this caution is ineffective, he shall repeat the above procedure and indicate to the Bowler that this is a final warning.

(c) Both the above caution and final warning shall continue to apply even though the Bowler may later change ends.

(d) Should the above warnings prove ineffective the Umpire at the Bowler's end shall:

(i) At the first repetition call and signal "no ball" and when the ball is dead direct the Captain to take the Bowler off forthwith and to complete the over with another Bowler, provided that the Bowler does not bowl two overs or part thereof consecutively. See Law 22.7: (Bowler Incapacitated or Suspended during an Over).

(ii) Not allow the Bowler, thus taken off, to bowl again in the same innings.

(iii) Report the occurrence to the Captain of the batting side as soon as the Players leave the field for an interval.

(iv) Report the occurrence to the Executive of the fielding side and to any governing body responsible for the match who shall take any further action which is considered to be appropriate against the Bowler concerned.

9. The Bowling of Fast High Full Pitches

The bowling of fast high full pitches is unfair. See Note (e). In the event of such unfair bowling the Umpire at the bowler's end shall adopt the procedure of caution, final warning, action against the Bowler and reporting as set out in 8. above.

10. Time Wasting

Any form of time wasting is unfair.

(a) In the event of the Captain of the fielding side wasting time or allowing any member of his side to waste time, the Umpire at the Bowler's end shall adopt the following procedure:

(i) In the first instance he shall caution the captain of the fielding side and inform the other Umpire of what has occurred.

(ii) If this caution is ineffective he shall repeat the above procedure and indicate to the Captain that this is a final warning.

(iii) The Umpire shall report the occurrence to the Captain of the batting side as soon as the Players leave the field for an interval.

(iv) Should the above procedure prove ineffective the Umpire shall report the occurrence to the Executive of the fielding side and to any governing body responsible for that match who shall take appropriate action against the Captain and the Players concerned.

(b) In the event of a Bowler taking unnecessarily long to bowl an over the Umpire at the Bowler's end shall adopt the procedures, other than the calling of "no-ball", of caution, final warning, action against the Bowler and reporting as set out in 8 above.

(c) In the event of a Batsman wasting time (See Note (f) other than in the manner described in Law 31: (Timed Out), the Umpire at the Bowler's end shall adopt the following procedure:

(i) In the first instance he shall caution the Batsman and inform the other Umpire at once, and the Captain of the batting side, as soon as the Players leave the field for an interval, of what has occurred.

(ii) If this proves ineffective, he shall repeat the caution, indicate to the Batsman that this is a final warning and inform the other Umpire.

(iii) The Umpire shall report the occurrence to both Captains as soon as the Players leave the field for an interval.

(iv) Should the above procedure prove ineffective, the Umpire shall report the occurrence to the Executive of the batting side and to any governing body responsible for that match who shall take appropriate action against the Player concerned.

11. Players Damaging the Pitch

The Umpires shall intervene and prevent Players, from causing damage to the pitch which may assist the Bowlers of either side. See Note (c).

(a) In the event of any member of the fielding side damaging the pitch the Umpire shall follow the procedure of caution, final warning and reporting as set out in 10 (a) above.

(b) In the event of a Bowler contravening this Law by running down the pitch after delivering the ball, the Umpire at the Bowler's end shall first caution the Bowler. If this caution is ineffective the Umpire shall adopt the procedures, other than the calling of "no-ball", of final warning, action against the Bowler and reporting as set out in 8. above.

(c) In the event of a Batsman damaging the pitch the Umpire at the Bowler's end shall follow the procedures of caution, final warning and reporting as set out in 10 (c) above.

12. Batsman Unfairly Stealing a Run

Any attempt by the Batsman to steal a run during the Bowler's run-up is unfair. Unless the Bowler attempts to run out either Batsman—see Law 24.4: (Bowler Throwing at Striker's Wicket Before Delivery) and Law 24.5: (Bowler Attempting to Run Out Non-striker Before Delivery)—the Umpire shall call and signal "dead ball" as soon as the Batsmen cross in any such attempt to run. The Batsmen shall then return to their original wickets.

13. Players' Conduct

In the event of a player failing to comply with the instructions of an Umpire, criticising his decisions by word or action or showing dissent, or generally behaving in a manner which might bring the game into disrepute, the Umpire concerned shall, in the first place report the matter to the other Umpire and to the Player's Captain requesting the latter to take action. If this proves ineffective, the Umpire shall report the incident as soon as possible to the Executive of the Player's Team and to any Governing Body responsible for the match, who shall take any further action which is considered appropriate against the Player or Players concerned.
NOTES

(a) The Condition of the Ball

Umpires shall make frequent and irregular inspections of the condition of the ball.

(b) Drying of a Wet Ball

A wet ball may be dried on a towel or with sawdust.

(c) Danger Area

The danger area on the pitch, which must be protected from damage by a Bowler, shall be regarded by the Umpires as the area contained by an imaginary line 4ft./1.22m. from the popping crease, and parallel to it, and within two imaginary and parallel lines drawn down the pitch from points on that line 1ft./30.48cm. on either side of the middle stump.

(d) Fast Short Pitched Balls

As a guide, a fast short pitched ball is one which pitches short and passes, or would have passed, above the shoulder height of the Striker standing in a normal batting stance at the crease.

(e) The Bowling of Fast Full Pitches

The bowling of one fast, high full pitch shall be considered to be unfair if, in the opinion of the Umpire, it is deliberate, bowled at the Striker, and if it passes or would have passed above the shoulder height of the Striker when standing in a normal batting stance at the crease.

(f) Time Wasting by Batsmen

Other than in exceptional circumstances, the Batsman should always be ready to take strike when the Bowler is ready to start this run-up.

INDEX TO THE LAWS OF CRICKET